by Edward Dorn

POETRY

The Newly Fallen (1961)
Hands Up! (1964)
Geography (1965)
Idaho Out (1965)
North Atlantic Turbine (1967)
Twenty-Four Love Songs (1969)
Songs Set Two—A Short Count (1970)
Recollections of Gran Apacheria (1973)
Collected Poems (1975)
Manchester Square (with Jennifer Dorn) (1976)
Hello, La Jolla (1978)
Yellow Lola (1981)
Captain Jack's Chaps (1983)
Gunslinger (1989)
Abhorrences (1990)

PROSE

By the Sound (1971, 1991)
Some Business Recently Transacted in the White World
      (1971)

NONFICTION

The Shoshoneans (1966)
      (with photographs by Leroy Lucas)

TRANSLATIONS (with Gordon Brotherston)

The Tree Between Two Walls (1969)
Our Word (1968)
Cesar Vallejo Selected Poems (1975)

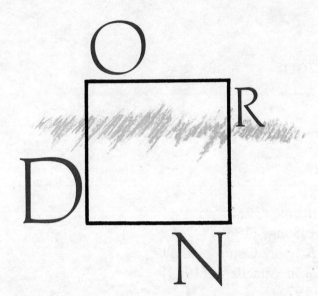

BY THE
SOUND

WITH A NEW PREFACE BY THE AUTHOR

EDWARD
DORN

BLACK SPARROW PRESS / SANTA ROSA / 1991

Black Sparrow Press books are printed on acid-free paper.

LIBRARY OF CONGRESS CATALOGING-IN-PUBLICATION DATA

Dorn, Edward.
  [Rites of passage]
  By the sound / Edward Dorn.
     p.   cm.
  Previously published as: The rites of passage.
  ISBN 0-87685-841-8 (cloth) : — ISBN 0-87685-840-X (pbk.)
  : — ISBN 0-87685-842-6 (signed cloth) :
  I. Title.
PS3507.073277R58   1991
813'.54—dc20
                                        91-19033
                                        CIP

CONTENTS

PREFACE

I arrived along with my associates, in the SKAGIT VALLEY IN 1957. THAT WAS BEFORE ELVIS WAS FAT. That was before the dead were Dead. That was when the Germans were divided—the East Germans were all Stasi and had infiltrated every cranny of the West German American puppet. That was before the propaganda of want—which crowded out the circumstances of human affinity. That was when everybody was under the same bleak outlook, no inside trades, no vomiting into the system of purely verbal claims; '29, the year I was born, was still a warning to '59. Eisenhower himself hadn't even seen the complex, and was using the Marines to quell disorder in the Lebanon—ironically to be the running sore, a diabetes of the American soul for America thenceforth, unto the present day.

How appropriate. How timely. How repetitive, how redundant, and how really tedious. By 1958 we were picking up fruit from the trees along the road—as part of our diet. The last vestige of nomadic habits colliding with modern waste. The sophistication in a time that is now considered a crude joke amazes me as I look back at it. The prophetic strokes are astonishing. In 1957 *Atlas Shrugged,* a novel in which all creative people withheld their ideas, was published—the first "mind strike." That presages the involuntary striking out of the power of the mind in the present, nine years from the end of the 2nd millennium, a moment like the approach of the 1st, a time of great anticipation and reflection. In the late fifties, which was the final closing of the books on the second war and its turbulent aftermath, before the worrisome and nagging preoccupations of "the quality of life" with all the attendant reactions and petty animosities which come to define the putative present, life was a struggle which was not so over-amped that it couldn't be studied by anyone who didn't have a hole in their bucket. I never met anybody in those days who didn't know what time it was. Now nobody says anything. There are just occasional columns updating the numbers of the Homeless. The point being if you can still read, and you have the paper in your hand, and your hand isn't frozen, then You are probably not homeless, yet. If that's not Capitalism I don't know what is.

Yet in lots of other ways, it's just business as usual. Governor Faubus says fuck off to the Supreme Court and closes four high schools. Sherman Adams resigns after receiving oriental rugs from a Boston industrialist, a payoff by present standards that would look like Eddie Murphy accepting a raccoon coat from Geraldo. Presented by a professional redneck. The point now would be that everybody and everything is professional. Homelessness is a profession. One doesn't say a few words into the mike and pass on anymore, one is unhooked and there is a faction which will show up to hook one back up. Death has become an activity. A concept and practice heretofore unthinkable.

Once the meat was in the market, everybody who didn't own the market was a slave. *That* has not changed. The price? Well the price is what they can get. *Naked Lunch* is published, *Look Back in Anger* is released. The last document of the inquisition, and the first expression of the New Resentment—the revolt of the masses discovers class—a cheap import from the south. Later, there would be Gender which was to become ideology without sex. Twin Peaks indeed. Voyeurism for those who don't remember that J. Edgar Hoover was the first official American Gay.

But such analysis was beyond the ken of the 1958 man or woman. There was a widespread knowledge that life was bad, who could miss that? Struggle for those who had no dividends was obvious. There were no grants and there was no representative coprophilia, and anyway shit had no special meaning for the underclass (even then, way prior to American propaganda of French restructuring) and no one sensed that, far in the future when Black would be abandoned for hemispheric designations, African-American would carry the seed of The Problem. Words are the true, the basic, molecular biology. Even the perfectly cloned will understand this.

Oecology doesn't know what it's missed. Back then the owls were as big as barn doors and they'd carry off your children. Nobody wanted to save a creature like that. The logging trucks were something else. The instance when the child of someone you knew wandered onto the route of giant Christmas Toy logging trucks and got smashed like a worm, red blood instead of green chlorophyll displaying the diet of an infant carnivore on the route of the log traffic through town, Tarheel recklessness, warfare of wages. The same stock which fueled the Korean "conflict" and which went to Vietnam and sewed dope into cadavers, and who loved the orphans they had created. Ah now they've gone to Saudi.

Everybody has heard of the translation into Something Japanese of the raw timber, cedar, hemlock, the prime spruces and firs of the Canadian and American coast above Prince Rupert. Business has made a mess of resources and the market has made product nobody needs and nobody wants—the intimidation to buy was categorical in Seattle in 1958. Horsemeat from Montana piled up like mountain ranges on the Pike Street market. In the Skagit Valley the slicks from plums and peaches and cherries dropped on roads caused accidents. There was no boom in Real Estate. Who would rush to a place where fruit was scattered on the ground in anarchic surplus? Importation has undoubtedly replaced that fallen fruit. And for every spruce tree and giant cedar slain and exiled to Japan there is a petroleum replacement predestined for the dump that as a people and a place we have become. *By the Sound,* masquerading as a "novel," is simply a sociological study of the basement stratum of its time: the never ending story of hunger and pressing circumstance in a land of excess.

Edward Dorn
February, 1991, Boulder

• 11

BY THE SOUND

JAMES STOPS BY

The Great Northern goes out of Seattle to VANCOUVER, B.C. SOMETIMES THE TRACKS RUN ALONG the shore of Puget Sound and where the shore line cuts abruptly west the rails continue across the arms of land, over the widening valleys of the Stillaguamish, the Skagit, and the Nooksack. All rivers coming down into the Sound. The countryside is drawn with a perpetual green. There are the haphazard growths of stump ranches and there are the old farms below those, on the tillable land. There is the slash left by the loggers on the slopes above. On the east Mt. Pilchuck stands grey and torn. Whidbey Island comes and goes for fifty miles outside the west windows of the train. Once in a while the winter storms take up the waters of the

Sound and cut away the ballast of the roadbed. The train slows then in the cold drizzle and the section crew stands aside. The travelers in the diner pause over their food or their drinks to express a fleeting interest. Every aspect of the land and sky is smudged. The cold, fine substance, more than mist, not quite rain, naturally haunts the atmosphere as it moves in slightly blown waves back and forth across the land and the islands.

The edge of the town is cool. The wet air is heavy today but the sun comes out of the overlap of clouds as it goes down. Then it flashed through a group of hemlocks across the vacant lot. The trees surrounded an old house and the rays diffracted into spikes and hit the hills for a few minutes making of the aluminum-sided grain elevator for a while a bright mirror. Then the sun was gone down into the Pacific, promising for tomorrow a clear day, which never came—and rarely did from such a sign—the light, feathery, rosy clouds of fair weather grew dim grey, the prevailing winds brought other clouds, dark, and dense with mist.

From the west the Sound could be smelled, felt on the wrists and neck, cold bands on the body. Carl Wyman watched the sunset from the window. Tomorrow they would continue packing.

It was mid-winter. The first of the year had passed. They were moving out. During the last week they had made elaborate but hasty plans which in the end will come to nothing more than what their lives had always been. They were tired. He could hear the children in the other room choosing the few toys they would be allowed to take, picking them up and dropping them, talking among themselves and sometimes making a game of the argument over the merits of what they each had.

James McCarty came in the morning. He came walking down the middle of the gravel road. A tall man, smiling, a slight lurch in his body, his chest caved in by a disease of the muscles. This unconformity was hardly noticeable but gave a strangeness to his walk. He came with an easy feeling of self-confidence, reflected in his smile, but the whole pose was finally tinged with insolence. He was a desperately poor man at times, and when he worked at his carpentry he drank. When he was out of work his tools were hocked, when he got work, he had to borrow money to redeem them. He had something of a talent for insult, which he enjoyed at his own expense because it kept him from getting work, his arrogance was not much appreciated by the union officials or his fellow workers. He arrived carrying a six-pack of beer and smoking a cigar.

The end of the packing was in sight. Three

trunks sat in the middle of the floor in the front room. The Wymans were glad to have this chance to sit around and contemplate their proceedings. James opened the beer. His hand curved around a bottle in a way peculiar to the subtle spasm that ran throughout his muscles. He held the bottle close up as he drank, his elbows pointed in toward his chest. But this appeared to be a mannerism of the way he sat rather than a malady.

This moment was a time familiar to all those who have moved from one place to another. A time when the greatest effort is over, when the packing is done, when all that is left is the game to be played: a pretense of "considering" what is to be taken and what left behind, and after everything small and in fact questionable, has been packed. The unmatchable sock slips through the fingers and one says philosophically, "leave it" with the same weight one says leave the washing machine. The Wymans are not poor by the strictest standards. After all they have the money to be gone. But on the other hand they don't have the money to move more than themselves and their few trunks and suitcases. They planned to go south, but since their destination was the cold high country, they would need something warm.

Well, here's to the trip, James said, I'll bet you'll never come back to this place. In fact, I'll bet you never

ever write to us. One thing's sure, you're lucky to be leaving. I hope we can get out of here soon, maybe down to California. That's the difference. You got the money to go. But if that dam job starts up in the spring, up at New Whalem, we might get out of here. If I can get my tools back in time. When do you think you can leave?

They replied that tomorrow or the next day seemed likely, but possibly that afternoon. There were still things they hoped to sell. Some of their things they planned to give to James and his wife, but some they wanted to leave with the Henderssons. There was the hot water heater someone could use, which, legally, should not be removed from the house. But they had installed it and felt it would do either the McCartys or the Henderssons much good to have it . . . Billy Hendersson was supposed to have come over that morning . . . it seemed a touchy business as to just how the division could be made. They grew uneasy as James began to make inquiries about the fate of certain things still lying around the house and in the barn. It became obvious that he was interested in all the desiderata. The fact is, the Wymans had not planned on the arrival of James McCarty. They had thought to get some things together to take out to the pea-shack before they left.

James now had the broom in his hand and was sweeping here and there, making an attempt to clean up. This seemed merely the occasion for a little reconnaissance of the rooms. He would disappear and then return suggesting something else that should be packed. But it was obvious that this suggestion clothed the hope that perhaps the article in question would not be shipped and that he could have it. At this point Carl and his wife, Mary, were pained by the realization that what would finally be left was not that important anyway, with the exception of the blankets. They were of strict value to anyone who lived as exposed to the disheartening elements of a northwest winter as did the McCartys and the Henderssons. But how to explain to James that a division was desired. He hardly knew of the Henderssons, and in the meantime there was the loyalty between the McCartys and the Wymans that had grown up during many hard times in the past. Their exchanges had been quite open and necessary. They had even divided at times their last two cups of flour.

James swept. When he picked up the screw driver and the pliers and put them in his back pocket the Wymans grew a little annoyed. They had planned to leave behind all such things, but there was still a need for the tools—the truck from the auction was to arrive in the afternoon to pick up the washing machine which had to be taken loose from the faucets. And the beds, they had to be taken apart. The small, undeterminable amount of money they hoped to receive from the auction people at the end of the first leg of their journey, when they would be staying with friends in Colorado. Carl opened another bottle of beer.

James again said he was very sorry not to be leaving too. You know, I'll never make it here. What construction work there is I can't always plan on anyway. Can you get your tools out of hock, Carl asked, Is the ticket still good? Yeah, I still got some time on it, oh hell yes . . . I'll get the tools. If I get fifty dollars. James let his head drop onto his chest. Carl had learned long ago this meant James was going to change the subject. It was just as well. Carl wished he had fifty dollars to give him, even if he did, it would mean taking James to the hock shop in Cedar Mills and seeing he got back to the pea-shack with the tools and then, as likely as not, they would be back in the shop the next day. Or that night. It didn't make any difference. But it could. It could. How? How could it. It could make a difference if he took this man's whole life in charge, saw that he got to the union every day, saw that he got to the job the first day, saw to everything. Oh goddamn, Carl thought, I can't start that again, I'm leaving this place at last, I can't think of anything else . . . but what will happen to them,

where will they be next year and the year after that . . .
But I'm lucky to be working for Smith. At least we can
buy some groceries, James said.

Do you think Smith will have something for you
to do the rest of the winter, Carl asked him. Yeah,
there's a lotta work to be done on those shacks before
the Mexicans come. That won't be long now . . .
Ramona and The Old Man are cutting back some
strawberry shoots right now, in the afternoons. Hell,
the pussy willows are out in that ditch back of camp,
did you know that? Jesus! That's pretty early. Yes it
is, Carl said. He thought yes, that's very early. It's like
that here. Everything, early and late, and hopeless and
hopeful and light and dark, mild and harsh . . . but
slow, everything slow and then in April there won't be
any more willow buds . . . what happens in April . . .
I can't remember. Probably nothing. Willow buds in
late January, out of their time. And James is working
off the one hundred and fifty dollar fine Smith paid to
get him out of jail, he's got him for that, absolutely.
Isn't that it . . . he'd never lend him the fifty to get his
tools out of hock, to get a regular job, no never! That
must be enlightened self-interest. Carl looked at James
and took a drink of beer.

Mary came into the room carrying some odds
and ends from the bedroom. She mentioned that there
would be about five months paid rent left on their cold

storage locker downtown. Did James think he could use it. He said probably so, but he couldn't think of what they'd put in it. Carl thought to himself as they talked what a poor suggestion that had been. The people who ran the locker plant would never allow James to use it. They were very used to the people they knew, coming and going. And it was not that James looked suspicious because he did not, unless you looked very close, and if you did that, he gave, finally, the unavoidable impression that he did not belong. Belong to what? Who knows. He just did not belong to anything. Perhaps not even to humanity as it is defined by merchants. Merchants have undeceivable eyes. They are the master seers. Everything they do is with their eyes. They are all eyes. One speaks of clothes, or of hardware, or of food, and in speaking of the entire class of "things" one must consult some sort of merchant. To whom all things at last come. It would be useless to give James the key, for unprotected, if he walked in to claim his proprietorship of the locker, he would be questioned. So simple a thing as what's your name. This was a small town.

It was getting on toward noon. The children had been asked not to go outside, they should have been in school and it was thought best that the neighbors know nothing of the departure.

The neighbors had been hostile from the

beginning. With the exception of a kindly old woman who was a character in the neighborhood, they had nothing to do with the Wymans. The house had been empty for five years before they moved in. It was little more than a shack. The surrounding houses were of the new tract type. The owner, who ran a lumber yard in the next town, was not very interested in it. He was holding the property for the land only; it was anticipated that when the east-west highway across the north to the Okanogan went through, it would go around the base of the hill in that town. That was where the house was.

Not far out of town on the road to Cedar Mills James lived in a pea camp. That part of the valley is horticultural. Fruit production amounts to less than does the cultivation of vegetables and berries. Of the vegetables the pea is most important. All along the littoral one will come across a field in the corner of which is pressed a little group of shacks which is called a pea camp. Not much space is spared for them, and their look is the same whether peas or berries are the question. The dimension of the shacks is fairly standard: about fifteen by twenty feet. There is usually a cookstove. From a distance a pea camp looks like a collection of small, windowless storage buildings, their shed roofs all pointed in the same direction. In this land of many trees there is rarely a tree in the camp. The area has not been planned with the occupants in mind—it has been assigned by the farmer for some unquestioned and unexplained reason of his own. The shacks are painted on the outside a green color, some collections bright, and some painted long ago. The inside air is close. There is usually no more than one window and that quite small. Perhaps two feet square. In this space large families live. Of course. People who do that sort of work, and who are expected to live sequestered from normal society, have large families. Sometimes in that small space there is a bunk arrangement for sleeping, tiers of double beds. Many sleep in a bed but often it is necessary for some to sleep on the floor. Mill scrap is burned in the stove. This wood is hauled in truckloads and is usually furnished by the landlord. It comes from the nearby logging towns, toward the mountains. As to whether or not all these people are charged rent for those hovels, it is difficult to say, and would seem probable that it varies, according to the personality of the landlord. Smith demanded rent for his—twenty dollars a month.

There are clusters of days when the dense mist verging on rain, yet not rain in the sense the man from the east will understand it, cuts the vision and shivers the body. When the temperature is in the thirties, one needs an extraordinary amount of clothing. Smoke curling from the many stovepipe chimneys parallels the ground and hangs there. It is wood smoke, so the smell is not bad, but the characteristic heaviness of everything, in which everything drips, has another effect. Days can go by in which there seems no variation whatever. If there is little hope to begin with, its undercutting will soon be accomplished.

James was something of a pack rat. As he swept he was naturally looking for things to carry off, regardless of their value, because it was a comfort. There is no attempt being made to deny the validity of this habit. When a man has nothing it would be senseless to censure him for petty thievery. Even major crimes are not so definable as they are said to be, many crimes are that only by definition of *who* is the transgressor. The point is that James also rifled empty houses for what he could find, and his stockpile of miscellaneous gear was prodigious. That fact is brought up simply because it bears directly on his existence in a pea-shack, that it made his being there more difficult because of space, and that he required two pea-shacks, and he lived generally in them only in the wintertime, when some were empty. He has recently gone back to work for a landlord named Smith at the rate of seventy-five cents an hour, and this landlord is not a pea grower at all, his fields are filled with strawberries.

THE CAMP

Ramona McCarty had five children. Three
OF THEM WERE WITH HER IN THE PEA-SHACK, THE TWO
others lived in foster homes in Seattle. Wards of the
State. Not much was known of the two in Seattle
because Ramona only talked about them when she was
passionately drunk. And drunk she got, at every
opportunity, and only as an Esquimau is able. So
deeply that the whole life of the organism seems
removed, or in her case, sheltered, from the
immediately outer world. There is a way of walking
they have, it is not the stumbling crashing
awkwardness, the thrashing desperateness of the
Irishman, but it is a great equilibrium in which their
thick bodies stilt upon the earth as they stay upright,

as though the earth's quake were its normal condition. Trainmen walk with a like authority.

But that she loved the children deeply and missed them a lot of the time, and thought about them as she went about her affairs, there is no doubt. There would be slight references in her talk that were never developed. And then she would smile slightly or draw on her cigarette and look away. It was in Seattle she first learned she had t.b. She was then married to a man, vaguely it was known of him that he had a respectable job, some kind of petty professional, perhaps an engineer at Boeing. Apparently he had not supported her well at all, though she spoke once of having lived in a house with a yard in the back of which were two apple trees. She had let the apples rot on the ground, perferring to buy those large Delicious apples from east of the mountains. One can suppose that at that time she was not a part of the Esquimaux in Seattle who wander around the forlorn stretches of lower 1st Avenue and Yestler Way, or along Occidental where the loggers' hiring halls are.

The end of that part of her life seemed to come when she got t.b. and went to a sanitarium. They told her she would have to spend a year in bed. She said, I'll be goddamned if I'll stay in bed a year! She had every night waited until the nurse passed by her room then climbed out the window to walk around the grounds.

She told herself that she would never again be able to walk if she did not use her legs. Talking about it later, she would laugh triumphantly, Can you see me a whole year in bed! One day as she lay in bed two women, welfare workers, came to tell her they were taking the children away from her. As she remembered it, they said she was not a good mother. These women just simply came in and told her they were taking her children—not that they were taking money from her husband to support the children while she was in the hospital thereby helping her to get well, they told her she wasn't a good mother. They told her she had to let them take the kids. There was nothing she could have done at that point anyway, her husband wanted a divorce. Ramona did not drink then. Each week she had gone to pick up her husband's paycheck. Because he was such a drunkard his habit was to drink all the money up. The man at the pay window always let her have the check. In the end, when she had met James and moved north, there were many parts of that dilemma left undissolved in her. The hazy feeling about the results of that time, and where she should start to sort the causes and the effects of it was one of her primary broodings. Her estimation of the stay in the hospital seemed to be this: the two women took her children and the doctors took one of her lungs. As if to satisfy those loose emotions she would go to Seattle from time to time to see the authorities, either by herself or with James, but either way would end in her getting drunk in some bar and then taking the lonely bus back north.

How and where she had first met James is not altogether clear either. In Seattle no doubt. And probably while drinking. It is not difficult to see why they attracted each other once one has gotten past the common ground of drink. Ramona is beautiful. Her face is large. The most forward character the mouth, her smile would begin in her eyes and finally by a slow passage end by engaging the whole lower part of her face, spreadabout and winsome. Her look was always a teasing disbelief. If the thing she gave her attention to were incredible she accompanied her smile with a little soft swearing. Her body on the other hand was of the kind it is hard to defend as appealing, or beautiful. At least to the conventional mind. Esquimaux are generally thick, and even squat. It is true she was heavily built. But not fat in the least. She was never more beautiful than when she made up her face in the old style with bright lipstick and rouge, using a little mirror from her pocketbook.

She was born near Nome. She had been educated to the twelfth grade at the Indian school and later she taught the lower grades. Certainly she spoke English very well and easily. Some habits she retained from her origin slightly embarrassed her. Once, in the Wymans' kitchen she noticed a large box of dog bones, scraps of meat and suet. Ooh, Davie look! In her enthusiasm she grabbed several pieces of the raw suet, gave some to her little boy, and they both ate it quickly and with obvious pleasure. Suddenly aware of what she had done, Ramona laughed and shrugged her shoulders. It would be difficult to say precisely when or why she first came down to Seattle from the north.

James was an arrogant man, perhaps beyond his power to make that quality secure. When he and Ramona had finished a night of drinking in a bar in town they would pile into the old car with no fenders and one headlight and head toward the camp. In that state, the process of getting in and out of the car was unbelievably slow. One might think they were merely waiting for help. They would both of them be alternately in front and behind the car, almost casual in their inability to enter. All the time talking very gently to one another yet sometimes saying quite ultimate things. James would tell her she was the worst, most filthy cunt he had ever known. His jealousy would range the most unlikely old men they had left in the bar, suggesting the most atrocious sexual posture she had allegedly met them in. She would smile deliciously and slowly groping her hand for the door handle, answer almost politely, You . . . Asshole. And then they would meet on some serious common ground consulting over what might have happened to the keys. Davie by this time may have awakened from his period of crying and sleeping, to smile, that most lovely smile he got from his mother, out the side window, smearing it, and laughing and jumping or holding his diaper up. The interior of the car in back had the seat removed and that was where the children rode. It was dirty beyond anything. Ramona, of course, was not dirty, nor, in other circumstances, were her children. She had the healthy but unformulated notion that cars were pigsties anyway and would never have considered them as things to be kept clean as one's abode. The individual who is primitive and only recently exposed to civilization grasps the intention of modern social form, and indeed he does desire most conventionally nearly everything, but clings with stubbornness to verities of that sort. There is no reason on earth why a car should be clean.

Yes, the radiance of her smile. And how she really did love to laugh. Stars in their systems were hardly more in accord than those two pastimes of hers. She was a flirt, it would do no good to deny it. What it led to is more difficult to say. James was right in his suspicions, though it was probably more often than not true that she was simply trying to extract beer from anyone who seemed susceptible.

When Davie was born they had not yet come up into the valley. They were staying in a house on Hood Canal. One of those rare snowstorms over Puget Sound came early in the evening. Ramona began to have pains, and they had no car, and the snow, deep and moist. They were caught. A certain self-assurance allowed James to think he could deliver the baby himself. Later, he talked of this delivery often, usually in connection with his own intrepidity, but also with the time spent in the cabin, which seemed to have been very pleasant and relaxed for them both. Davie was a healthy child, and was apparently able to withstand all amounts of filth where he found it, in the back of the car, in the washwater outside the washing shack at the camp. Knowing that he had been delivered by his father, one might have looked at him a little more closely. Their relationship, father and son, did not go much beyond that event. The father's attitude was one of casual indifference toward the boy, and must also have been at the time of the birth, at least it seemed plausible that the legs were grasped as described and the boy was waved in the air with a certain irrelevant pride, a few slaps, the cigar was laid momentarily aside, James smiled, and said, Well what about that, Ramona, who the hell do you think he'll look like, you or me. He doesn't look much like an Esquimau. He had cut the cord with a pair of scissors and tied a knot in it down close to the belly. Whereupon he very likely gave the child to Ramona, relit his cigar, and sat down in a chair with one of his used, borrowed, or scavenged adventure magazines, sitting very formally, his legs crossed, holding the magazine properly, his cheesecloth lumberyard cap on, one half the magazine rolled up behind the page to be read and held with one hand. And from time to time looked up, mumbling, smiling, laughing softly, and then put another stick of wood in the fire. But this was a moment for Ramona when her face took on its motionless blank cast, a brooding ground within her own mind where she met this utter failure of a white man, who delivered babies as he might turn on water taps or fix tires. Not gentle or ungentle, but highly matter of fact. Her own ambitions for a man were more conventional. After that delivery the last two children were born in hospitals, at a time when they had come to accept Welfare as the simplest way through an inconvenient time.

It must be understood that the entire demand of life changed for them in the valley. It is one thing to be in a comfortable cabin, another to be in a pea-shack. In the days after their arrival, James worked at one of the construction sites up close to the mountains. This was short-lived as most construction is, this particular job was a hydroelectric dam. One night when he was driving back down along the river there occurred an incident which seemed for him of equal weight and significance as attending Davie's birth. He was driving along and came to a curve, either fell asleep or was dulled from drinking, possibly both, when the car of its own choice left the road and started for the river through the slash of a logged area, miraculously missing all the cedar and fir and hemlock stumps which lay in the path like dark, looming boulders. The car entered the river from a bank over the cut of a bend and since there was no one around the splash of its impact was lost in the night. James stirred behind the wheel of the car, now totally submerged. He looked around the interior, rolled the window down, climbed out and rose to the surface. The current carried him down to the bank. Then he walked into town. He spoke of this affair very often with the conclusion: See, that's the difference. And whether one were really aware of it or not, there did seem to be a difference. A tale that has no more of the logic left in it.

It must have been fairly soon after the McCartys moved into the camp that Carl Wyman met James. The two had started talking as they sat next to each other in a bar. James was on his way to Seattle to see his mother. He spoke of his whole family down there, his father whom he could not stand, of his brother who lived nearby in the valley and was a surveyor, of his sister who was a nurse. His mother he liked very much. Carl was caught by a certain pretentiousness in the man's talk. The first machine out of his small arsenal was Friedrich Nietzsche, whose last name was pronounced with a slight explosiveness. If the effect of this were lost, as it mostly was in the taverns of that town populated by loggers, migrant workers, tramps and construction people, Immanuel Kant would appear. And there was Zola. And Socrates. Jack London. And then someone odd like Florence Nightingale. And then again, someone more believable, as Byron. But on those occasions it must be granted he spoke as if he had happily missed all the meetings of a great books course.

Although James and Carl did not see each other for several months after that, the two families eventually were drawn together by one or two common interests. The McCartys wanted desperately to get out of the pea camp. What made their predicament in that respect enduring was of course that they had hardly even the start of the means to accomplish it. The Wymans on the other hand were superficially better off in town. They were able to get up the small rent each month on the house. But Carl generally had no more work than James. The result was that although they both lived chronically on the edge of things, and that there was always the fine adjustment to be made between what they needed for a minimal kind of life and the necessities they could finally come up with, they both did have an odd and desperate leisure, which neither of them were willing to consider altogether bleak, and there were many times they fell into an enjoyment of their surroundings which would last for weeks on end.

Those people who are not quite poor in the most pressing sense, if they are constitutionally able, can enjoy their periods of unemployment. There is the local example of the telephone employee. By all odds his job is hard to come by, there being certain requirements, such as a kind of dependable residence and character, that always have to be satisfied. References are very "qualitative" things in a community composed of at least half a population that is unknown and therefore undependable. The pettiest of secure and dependable jobs becomes part of the usufruct of the established in the local society. The position, say, of telephone lineman, which would not even momentarily interest a man with the smallest particle of ambition, becomes known as a visionary thing to hope to get, there are known standing lists of fifty to a hundred men, which will never be used save as bait by the company for the reputation of an open policy, while in the meantime the opening, if it does occur, will go invariably to a nephew or cousin, if not to a son, and rarely even to a friend. Not to go into that here and now, it inevitably influenced the manner of unemployed life, and set beside the standardization of complaint against those who work only part of the year as being shiftless, the people of our narrative were forced into a kind of spiteful enjoyment of the spare time that came upon them.

And in respect to how such an enjoyment of a poor situation could be practised, a note on the weather. It is well known that the man who has not attached himself to something dependable in a cold climate is in for a miserable time. It is never quite possible to relax and run about in a rigidly cold climate unless one is dressed, fed, and housed properly. The thin populous edge of country between the Cascade Mountains and the Sound is not such a cold country. True, it is nasty, and nagging, and respiratory complications are common from the dampness which magnifies all cold; but there is no real danger because the temperature is never threatening in that way. The man who will freeze in the Yukon or in Minnesota is of course in real danger. But cold in other terms is simply an inconvenience. Rather it is wet there, and as has been suggested, many of the days are dark. It is a cyclone area. Large snows can come but do not usually. The interesting factors of the weather can become chamber of commerce coinage whether they are harsh or fair. Simply by the elimination of one extreme you have a talking point for the other. If people in that area said they were glad it did not snow, they were performing as expected, the damp is in no way superior to harsh dry cold, except in the sense of meaning ultimate danger. And of course most people who are sage about the weather have no stake in it.

When Mary Wyman visited Ramona, which was not often, Ramona would immediately put on water for tea. If there had been beer around Ramona would be drunk. The quiet times brought tea and reflective talk. One of their common ambitions was to move away from the places they lived in, so they talked of the possibilities of that. The children liked to play together, Davie was small enough to interest the Wymans' older children and he was delighted by the attention. So in the cabin they would sit, and sip tea and talk quietly. There were myriad cats around the camp and they came and went. Cats and tea. Many were the times in the afternoon the little shack was the pleasantest place in the world, crowded as it was inside, crowded as the building was in the camp. As Ramona moved in the shack she talked, and sometimes picked up one of the babies. Always there was that intense smiling gossip women take so much pleasure in. And there was no end of it in the small compressed community of the camp. It was more like a village in its compression than a community of one part and goal. There were sharp animosities. When Ramona had an interesting report to make she whispered. There were Indians, mostly Canadian, the bulk were Texas and California Mexicans, and a very few Esquimaux. The Esquimau and Indian had got there by a slow, irreversible reduction of the logging industry, until there was nothing more for them to do but commit themselves.

Often James would return from town or from work, and he would have groceries and cigarettes. When sober and feeling well he looked like a very young man. His greeting was usually Hi! and his interest in anyone there was casual and genuine, he had a way of nodding, saying yeah, yeah, rolling his cigar in his mouth and saying yup, or interjecting something in agreement very fast with a conclusion of happy affirmation. There was something about those times, those returns, those visits, that recall the coming home of Hansel and Gretel's parents, with flour and sugar, from the fortunate sale of their brooms. A darkness to the edge, a misfortune waiting in the background. There were those other times, when they were drunk and entering a place, or leaving, and then the endless battle with the car and the long slow drive home to who knows what coldness, to a bed and a place that was anything but prepared, to the brawling Mexicans and the drunk dead smiling Indians.

The few unattached poor white men who inhabited the camp were like ghosts. Their presence there could hardly be explained—they seemed derelicts of the spirit who had wandered off course and found it impossible to get back. There was one old man whom Ramona called The Old Man. He was small and frail, and he wore a brown hat. He was never expected to say anything and it was thought he never did. He smiled, as an answer to anything. But it never struck one as a habit, rather it seemed to be his true speech. He had a cat he loved very much, it slept around his neck. But one night he lost it. A small cat, slightly more than a kitten. On one of Mary's visits, Ramona mentioned that The Old Man had lost his cat. Late that night Carl took him one of their kittens. It was raining harder than usual, the beams of the car's lights shot into the camp like icicles filled with moving particles. James helped Carl find the cabin where The Old Man was staying. They went all about the camp knocking on doors answered by blank faces that had not expected callers, a sudden extended square of light falling on the ground at that moment they opened the door. But it was hard to say where The Old Man lived since he lived here and there, with anyone who felt it their duty to take him in, or as they fancied. He was adrift and that condition is so common with these people they accept it as a prescribed part of life and make no statutory distinctions. The Mexicans were more factional and exclusive. He stayed with Indians. They have no religion of elaborate delegation to dispose of such things as homeless white men. A general irony it is up to the ethnologist to probe.

But at last they found where he was staying and The Old Man was very glad to get the cat. The meeting was fully acknowledged and final, and he even nodded with his smile. Then he took the cat over to the bed and laid her down on the pillow. There was a girl of thirteen or fourteen years who thanked the two men profusely, backing away from the door and inviting them in, but they could not stay and so made apologies. Carl was very impressed by the graciousness of the Indian girl and would have perhaps entered, but James was nearly drunk and did not seem to care much beyond the mission at hand.

A TRIP

One day as Mary sat in the pea-shack
TALKING TO RAMONA IT WAS SUGGESTED BY ONE OR THE
other of them that they make a trip to the Sound to
dig clams. It would be a nice outing; the clams could
be baked right on the beach, in the shell. They decided
to leave early. The next morning the McCartys drove
into town and they all left in the Wymans' car which
was in a little better condition. This excursion, though
acknowledged by none of the adults, was also to be
made the occasion to look for houses in the country.
Unacknowledged because none of them imagined they
could rent or buy one if they found it, but it was one
of the diversions that made up their hopes.

The countryside approaching the Sound is a

miscellany of quaintness. Sometimes the ugly remains of old logging operations. Small clearings. Stump ranches. As they rode along they talked and laughed, admiring the neat arrangement of one house as against what could be done with another. Ramona occasionally coughed violently, smiling when she recovered herself. Sometimes she swore softly, Goddamnit. And on they rode. There were many empty houses. At one time not so far back they were homesteads. They were large. They would be of no interest or use except to men who live in structures far worse. James was endlessly interested in them. It was a subtle matter to tell if he simply wanted to rifle through them, or was thinking of moving in. It was commonly known about these houses that they were not for let under any circumstances, but in a few cases they could be fixed up to meet what the owner thought an advantageous exchange for himself.

The appearance of these persons was not of the sort a farmer would put confidence in. The Wymans indeed had had an interview with a farmer about one of these empty houses. They found who owned it and had called the man, arranged to talk to him about seven o'clock in the evening. The man lived in one of those very large white houses with a small barn in the back which had a cupola and weather vane on top. At the edge of town. Nearly everyone had seen such a house.

A daughter was there. They met in a large diningroom. All the windows were clean. The man's wife had passed away, the daughter and the mood of the house verified that. The daughter was anxious after his affairs but could obviously save her energy, unless she had nothing else to do, for he was one of those capable old men. To the end, which was nearly there for him, he would keep that alertness which turns small amounts of money into an accumulated world of its own. In short, he questioned Carl about the work he did, and upon learning the work was of an indefinite nature, and more importantly, infrequent, he asked him what plan he had for fixing up the house. When Carl had to reply in the most hesitating words, however sincere, because he did not have the money to make immediate orders for material, the man smiled. The daughter was less demanding, she thought it might be an interesting enterprise, probably seeing in Carl at least a bottomless pool of free labor. As she sat at the table she swung her crossed leg, and flung her hair in a most interesting way. It may have been she was an unmarried real-estate agent. But it all ended with the man saying he would think it over, and with that he so conclusively smiled that there had been no mistaking the end of the interview.

As they rode along the gravel roads with thick close second growth on both sides, they came to a place the Wymans thought they recognized as the entrance in to the Henderssons' place. Their house, an unfinished shack in the woods, lay about a quarter of a mile back in the dense green growth and was quite impossible to see from the road.

They were heading for the highway that follows the Sound, it is a twisting elevated road but affords a nice view of the islands and, at least in the winter, is not very traveled. Carl thought of a house he had once seen from a distance and was sure was not lived in. It was over on the Sound and looked to have been an old boat house from where he had stood on the road. He said that they all ought to go over and walk up to it. Everyone agreed.

When the sun broke out full from behind a cloud they were nearly there. The house sat not far back from a levee that ran for some distance around a small inlet of the Sound. The tide was low. The children ran along the top of the levee toward the boat house which itself was as generous as a barn. The four adults walked slowly, taking in this structure which with each step showed itself to be more interesting than it had from the road. At last they were on the levee walking along a path bordered by delicate winter weeds. The wind blew them as one frail wall for yards ahead. They walked single file. Ramona asked breathlessly if the others thought the owner was nearby and might be watching. She was nervous. James was speculating on who would own such a place, and what their reasons would be for not using it some way. He thought it must be someone like a doctor from Seattle, or Vancouver. That made sense.

There was no other house close by. Some of the fields in back, which stretched across the flat coastal plain toward the mountains were under cultivation. Off to the northwest there was a full bright view of Mt. Baker, its squarish top shone white now under the sun. The house was three stories high. All the windows had been broken except for a few small panes high up. The glass lay strewn in very tangible confusion about the house. The children were cautioned about it. They wandered around the place. The space was enough to set their imaginations going. If they had been able to see the wreckage hunters and small boys had made with their guns, and vandals had made in their boredom, they would have been different people. What they saw was the great bulk of the main house which must have accounted for twenty rooms, and then were even more impressed by the spaciousness of what looked to be two bunkhouses that went off in a right angle from each other in the back.

James was the most enthusiastic. The carpenter allowed that it would be a great job, but the house could be restored. He carefully omitted to say it would take a lumberyard to repair a place this size. He did say, Imagine that, how many people do you think you'd be able to invite here, Jesus, just think, you could put up thirty people in the bunkhouses alone, and you could have a boat, wow, look at those flats, there must be a lotta clams in there, I'll bet this place hasn't been clammed out. And man those cookstoves are in good shape, you could use those, did you see, there's four cookstoves and six heating stoves in there. You know, I'll bet nobody's ever come back here, you could grow a garden, and have a boat, and never have anything at all to do with all those pricks out there. Ramona asked with a scowl, Why don't you want anyone to come back here, what do you mean, huh, and what would you do anyway for food you big nut, you can't grow everything in a garden. I want to go to town once in a while. Oh James, you always talk like that. And he answered her by asking her if she wanted to stay in that pea-shack the rest of her life living like an animal. Animals, he said, they live in places like that. She fell silent, because she really did not agree or disagree with him. She was teasing him a bit.

They walked around the grounds of this fabulous shambles, discussing the ins and outs of what it might mean to live in it, but the reality of any proposal to inhabit it did not make an incursion in their thoughts. As it turned out they did approach the man

some weeks later who had the rent of the fields sur-
rounding the place. He said he had hay in the barns
and was very much afraid of fire, but uppermost in his
mind was a suspicion that if anyone wanted to live in
that house there must be a thing or two about them
that was not quite right. A lawyer in Seattle owns it,
the farmer said.

That day they did not go clam digging. By the
time they got back into the car it was well after noon,
so they decided to take a long way home instead. They
drove back down the country road along the Sound.
When an empty house appeared they were always in-
terested, but it had become a half joke and they just
played the game. They never knew why it was beyond
them to have such a place. That no one else wanted
it, obviously, made it seem possible to have. It had been
a grand place, the possibility of having the remnants
of that grandness appealed to them, yet some instinct
told them to forget it.

These people are possessed by the weirdest of
modern ambitions. For the man without means to seek
a private space for himself would be a nightmare if
encountered in a dream. Even the middle-class man
who has at least some encouragement for his aims
instinctively knows that the world has already gone a
long way in contracting for the curtailment of any
untoward movement. Not even to say any abrupt

movement. It is as though a snake waits to strike. This syndrome is more clearly manifest in the western United States. There being more land there, the hope of that old possibility, the rancorous man who sees security in space, lingers on. It is a well-known marvel that one can travel great distances there, through uninhabited land, which nonetheless is mysteriously owned. But these people are casual victims, and not too much should be made of it. They have other problems.

Happily at last, and a few weeks after that day, the McCartys located a nice little place in the country, and the arrangement for it was the best one, James was to make minor repairs for the rent. They would be able to leave the pea-shack. There were four rooms downstairs and two above. It was not far off, three miles at most, from the camp. Ramona told Mary there were some fruit trees in the yard. She smiled, and drew on her cigarette, and looked at Mary for a long time, making the very natural heart of her smile, and then she said, Some of the cherry trees are Queen Anne's.

The Early Days

The Wymans came to the valley because
OF WHAT THEY THOUGHT WAS A PRESSING NEED TO LEAVE
the city although as time passed they saw this pressure
had been largely of their own construction. Carl's old
friend was then working as a rigger at a lumber camp
based at Fergesson, a village in the upper valley. Carl
had been hired on this man's word. The logging lasted
through that first summer and then there was a general
cutting back of the new men in the Fall, and Carl was
out of work.

For a while Carl stayed at home. The house
needed some fixing; the roof leaked, some of the
foundation was loose. He made trips to pick up cedar
scrap to burn in the stove. The only advantage with

cedar was that it was free, otherwise it was difficult to handle and sparked so tremendously it was dangerous to remove the stove lids. The wood was so liable to take in moisture that even when it had been dried, and sheltered, a wet day would infuse it with dampness again, making it very difficult to burn. When dry the chopping of it was dangerous. It had a latent spring and sometimes both pieces would fly into the air. Once Mary came to the back door to find Carl knocked cold by a piece that had flown up against his forehead. This sort of life was new to them, and they did not always laugh about it, but generally they were quite satisfied with where they were. The lack of work was their most constant worry.

They read a great deal and tried to keep the fire going. These were quiet days. Later, when they were preparing to leave they would think of the time they spent in this country as having been three years, but it was exactly a year and a half. There was not that adjusted pace which makes some lengths of time seem perfectly in accord with what has happened. They were pressed closely to gather fuel, food, or make compromises in a thousand ways for alternatives to what called for money. They arrived in July.

There was a small barn in back of the house close under the hill. Someone gave them a pair of rabbits, and since there were hutches there already, they raised them. At first Carl found it so difficult to finally kill one for food that the rabbits multiplied beyond feeding them. Some were turned loose. After a while, as things pressed the family more, Carl killed them a little more easily if no less anxiously. He could never stand the soft cracking sound the skull made when it was struck with a club. And the awful expectancy of the rabbit which grew into what he thought was a cognizance between himself and the animal. After hitting one he would throw it violently into a far corner of the barn on the hay and turn from it with a retch. Sometimes the rabbit would not be killed and he would then have to go over to finish it off, at which times he would hit it too hard and too much. It was as if the rabbit had suddenly turned into a threatening thing, something to be escaped from at all cost, and it worried him at times that he might not be able to curb the frenzy of his hitting it. He thought that he did not hate the rabbit in those moments. But he knew that fear and hate are incestuous. Though it occurred to him he naturally rejected the solution that someone has to kill those animals destined to be eaten, so why not himself, since it is smug to hire butchers to do it. He was not self-deceiving about that.

One late afternoon toward the end of September Carl took a walk along the road that wound to the top of the hill in back of their house. As he arrived at each switchback he stopped, at each turn the view was greater, and when he finally reached the top he stood for a while looking at the small cars cross the tracks by the WhileAway tavern. The aluminum grain elevator glistened in the evening light. Far to the right the road ran straight northwest toward the Sound and eventually was lost in the mist. His thoughts wandered like a purposeless dog stopping here and there, from the city and his friends to the valley and the people he knew off in the brush under the struggling smoke of their cabins. Logging trucks moved down from the mountains toward the main highway. Workers poured in their cars down from the mountains through the town, loggers, construction workers from the new power dams. In front of him beyond the town he could see the shine on the water of the Skagit where it bent toward the salt marsh. After a while he started down. He was supposed to kill a rabbit for their dinner but instead of going to the hutches by the barn when he reached the house, he sat down on the back steps. He lit a cigarette and breathed deeply. The clouds were rolling in from the west black with rain. The earth was darkening.

Killing the chickens bothered him less and he thought now about why that was. He had been raised on a farm in Illinois. It was impossible for him to remember exactly how many times he had seen his mother wring the neck of a young rooster or old hen. It must have been several hundreds. He could still see her come out of the chicken house with the bird under her heavy arm, the thing would calm down slowly with short nervous sounds from its throat, a mixture of clucking and rasping gasps from its beak, almost a part of its breathing. Sometimes she would let him hold it and he could feel its swift heartbeat. He could control the frenzy of its squawking.

He would feel its feet. The hard bright yellow scales and the claws, and the darker yellow around the rough sole. While he waited for his mother to get the boiling water he would pet the head, and put his finger in the claws. If the chicken did not take hold of his finger he would bend its leg and force it gently, the same with the legs his mother gave him when they were cut off. And when his mother returned from the house he would always hand her the chicken with his arms thrust out. Chickens seemed completely predictable, they always gave the same start, made the same throaty noise if you moved them, and turned in a slow arc, the head seemed detached as it revolved upright, always true to the earth like a gyroscopic compass, the eyes unchanging as the brown grey lid covered them off and on with

some ancient lingering periodicity of sleep. He waited
for this. He looked at his mother as a small boy
looks at anything large, at the horizon; he tried to
look at her but the picture was green and black, the
soil and the corn, and a touch of red from the barn.
He waited for the thing to dance into his circle of
vision, white, drenched with red around the stump
of the neck. Sometimes she dropped it before the
head came off and then silently swore, damn it, going
impatiently to catch hold of it again. Those were
terrible moments, deliciously compelling, and he
danced and screamed and sometimes ran behind a
tree to look out. The thrill of pain in him, the desire
to run after it, grab it, tear it, put its head back on
to see if the eyes would work, to see if it would be
able to walk around again and peck at the ground
and run in a chicken's heavy side to side way. Some-
times when he played he imitated a running chicken.
When he lay in the red barn on the ears of corn he
would think of his own neck wrung off and try to
feel if he would jump around squirting blood in all
directions over the green grass. If he were walking
out to play and came across a chicken head on the
ground he invariably picked it up and pulled the eyelids
back, opened the beak and felt the tongue. Sometimes
he would put it in his pocket.

When the hot days came he spent much of

his time lying around in one or another of the barns. The implement shed far out back was by the pig pens. Their slow grunts and squeals and the dust they made rise would lull him into a fantasy about animals or faraway places. The space in the barns was like an immense peaked vault, the rafters seemed like ribbing. There were many cracks and holes in the shingle roof. The shafts of the sun coming through picked up the dust from the rooting of the pigs. Most often there was a chicken or two picking around for seeds and bugs in the loose dirt as he entered the barn. They would scurry out of the way squawking but less urgently than when they were about to have their necks wrung. He tried to recall now, yes. It was the Winters' Place. The first dim fantasies of sex came to him in the deep stillness of the barns. It was there on that farm his family thought they were in for better days. Before that his father had worked for a farmer who lived in a big house, it had seemed like a manor house with its many bedrooms upstairs, and closets, its huge porches, and his family had occupied a small three room house nearby. When they moved it was to the house he was thinking of now, a house apart, with an upstairs too, and four or five miles away from the farmer, who had leased several farms, with men on each of them to care for them. He thought suddenly what has this to do with animals. Oh yes, I was in the barn when my father came around the side of the shed suddenly and pulled down his pants.

Carl sat down on the damp steps of the porch. Come to think of it, on that other place, it might have had something to do with Mrs. Daly. The 7th grade? No idea of masturbating, or any direct stimulation. Dreaming about Mrs. Daly. Some sense of what it was. In fact, that's what that place was. Then the Winters' Place. A year, no, two years. She gave him twelve and a half cents an hour to clean out her chicken houses. He kept the money in a tin can under his bed and sometimes accumulated two or three dollars. He couldn't remember doing the work. But the money. They were so poor his mother would borrow the money to get groceries on Saturday night. She'd go to town, they'd all go, and park in front of a store called the Grab-It-Here, everyone called The Grab-It. A ten pound sack of flour and some beans and two pounds of oleo. He liked to break the little package of color and mix it. But what's that? What useless debris, he thought. He was thinking about animals. It seemed a fixed cluster. Horses, the smell of their sweat which he liked, the smell of pig dung, which he didn't like except mixed with dust and then because, no it wasn't because he liked it but because the dust seemed identifiable and in one place. And the pigs openly fucking, that always embarrassed him, the same way his masturbating made him feel uncomfortable. Oh what bullshit! It's just that damn debased relationship raising animals. Feeding, eating animals.

I look at animals and I think of my own life. A rabbit's eyes reflect my own life back to me. That can't be true. When I look into those eyes I am reminded, that may be. Reminded of other times I've been with them, around them, touched by them in some way. Hit in the goddamn head. Dogs for Christ's sake are not it, a kind of arbitrary equality, a dog suffering all my own devices, a reflection in the eyes. No. With other animals it is different, you look into the eye, and the look keeps going down down down. A deathless stillness of penetration, there is no end, there is just the going on and on. Or pigs reflect the surface too, give it back like dogs, but with pigs you know they know what they're doing. Their tails are curled but they do not wag.

The poverty, the smells, the shame, what I remember of girls I wanted, too late. Dreaming of Mrs. Daly, our vicious connections on her stairs, rolling around on the landing. Saving the money in the tin can, giving it to my mother to buy groceries, her pleasure at getting it, my good feeling, after a while, that it was there for her. I was ashamed then when I thought to keep the money and walk to town and spend it, and hide the thing I got.

All those farms went together like connected boxes. Mrs. Daly. Her husband had not been like the other farmers his father had worked for. Mr. Daly had attended the University of Illinois agriculture school. All the other farmers were just like his father except they owned the farms and were very well off and drove around in the fields seeing about things and his father worked hard and was tired at night. His father got sixty dollars a month and two hogs to butcher in the Fall for his labor. But all of them, including Mr. Daly, would stand and listen to his father tell them how things were going, with their hands on their hips, their heads down, digging their toes in the plowed soil or breaking up clods with the soles of their shoes. His father seemed to know so much, Carl always listened to his talk with great attention, as he explained with such detail and such patience, and the bosses would say a few words about what to do tomorrow. Carl wondered why they owned things, barns, fields, animals, cars, tractors, trees, wagons, and his father didn't. Of course he knew. He knew . . .

Mrs. Daly, he had been told, had a special place in her heart for him. He must have behaved obnoxiously around Mrs. Daly, he thought. She had been as important in his life as Little Orphan Annie,

Captain Midnight, and Jack Armstrong. What was her first name? He didn't remember. Clara? No, something like that . . . she would, well, how was it . . . they would be in a frame of his dream. Still. Endlessly staring at each other and he *knew* she loved him and he got a sexual feeling out of it. The stairs, yes, that usually happened on the stairway in her house at the end of a busy day together. It seemed like pure hot love. It couldn't have been vivid sexual encounters we had, but I did have the sense we were coupled there on the stairs, not like the *experience* of it, but I was in her somehow, and she was warm and nice and comforting. I woke up from those dreams exhausted. All the years he spent on the farm there was never, except once, a girl his own age around. There was just nothing to do on that farm that wasn't extreme . . . watching the rats shot on Sunday morning, cleaning the chicken houses, driving the team of horses when his father let him. It was an isolated, confusing time. The thousands of rats in the corn-crib. Mr. Daly and his son shot them for an hour or so on Sunday morning. Jim, the son, ate his breakfast sitting out under the tree with his rifle across his legs waiting for the rats to run out from under the crib. He cut the feet off the ones he shot and took them to high school . . . it had something to do with a Future Farmers of America project. It was all mixed up, rats, horses, chickens, Mrs. Daly with her apron on, her soft hair on top her head—one gold tooth in front. Twelve and a half cents an hour. The lamb that was infested with maggots over its entire back quarters, the wool fallen away. The holes where the maggots went in and out and the lamb, until it dropped dead, running around slightly nervous as if it could find no place to rest. Mr. Daly and his son had experimented with various solutions of creosote and lye which they poured over the lamb to kill the maggots. The worms wiggled out when they poured the black liquid into the holes but there were too many, the lamb was a living hive.

That was years ago. But he had grown up with animals . . . that time in the implement shed . . . when he saw his father at the end of the breezeway with his pants down, doing his job. Carl was sitting on the iron seat of a hay rake. He watched his father's every move without speaking. He was afraid. When his father left, Carl went to the end of the shed and looked at the steaming pile left in the sun, a few flies had found it. Sparrows flew in and out of the breezeway, it was very still. He felt the familiar loneliness and alarming quiet of the barn. He ran away from it back toward the house.

It was a favorite game, standing in the barn, in the middle if he felt cool, by the door if he didn't, waiting until the silence became unbearable, looking at the cracks of light in the roof, and then running toward the house and getting there out of breath, entering the house and trying to control his lungs so he could talk to his mother in a calm way about some trivial thing he'd noticed here or there. Sometimes he did this after he was spent with masturbation and then in mock innocence he would ask her what it was she'd asked him to do, pretending some helpfulness. He did these things when he was startled, wandering in and out of the barns. He always felt a latent danger and gloom in those dusty buildings. If the noises of the animals stopped for more than a few seconds he was terrified. In high afternoon everything was asleep, his mother was asleep, only the slightest sound occasionally came from the tractor moving across the horizon, a faint red or orange thing creeping so slowly back and forth he could barely tell it moved. That was the ill-omened time of day. A crow dropping from tree to fence post, a single grasshopper with a rapid dry click moving over the grass.

His mother was aware of his fear and she amused herself in those days telling him stories of weird men who stayed in the barns. They were like the shadows, you couldn't tell them apart. They were strangers. One of the first real books she had read to him was *Robinson Crusoe.* He thought of the habit he still had—looking for strange footprints around the doors of buildings he was about to enter.

But the killing of animals had always bothered him. He watched the men shoot the pigs and cut their throats with their pocket knives. It gave him a strange jump in the pit of the stomach when they castrated the piglets, when the spurt of blood came out with the testicle and the cords pulled tight were then quickly cut.

It was that damn meanness he connected with everything in his life. His father forever so tired and skinny looking. His mother starting every supper they ever ate telling the old man they couldn't go on like that, that he had no spunk, as she put it, the farmer was just using him, he was too *soft,* that was another of her favorite words. He looked at him often, trying to figure out what she meant by that. He seemed so hard, and lean, you could see the knots of muscle in his thin arms. He took his supper with his head bent, his elbows on each side of his plate, chewing slowly, swallowing with difficulty, the permanent dirt under his nails, his forehead pale white above the line of his cap, the lower part of his face dark with the endless touch of the sun. His voice was low and precise, with a slightly hurt tone, a formal hitch, a clearing of his throat, and then some reasonable but slightly pleading thing would come out.

The regular Sunday trips in the old car. Always to visit someone a few miles away and then he would put on his dress shirt and his hat and his pair of stiff dress pants. The comments along the way about the height of the corn in the different fields they passed, how so and so's oats were coming. The same thing every Sunday. An interest in the progress of the affairs of those who owned things. An absolute meanness of interest they were unaware of. Utter defeat and utter hopelessness. The feeling of being isolated like a small band of slaves inside a completely legal trans-action. Even the animals were superior. They had that allotted time before they grew fat enough for the market.

But Carl had hated his father for his helplessness without knowing anything about him. Was his father then the rabbit you could knock in the head and walk away from? Without one shred of remorse look back on as the man kicked in the dirt, and return to finish him off? He had hated him abstractly. His mother encouraged that in spite of herself. With her digs at him she must have covered the entire range of her own fruitlessness. But there it is. The meanness they lived in ruled them, was their boss, those men who owned them simply came across the fields toward "their" lives as the agents between them and their simple, tentative existence. They hardly knew they were alive. They hardly felt it. Even the sharp edge of real poverty was taken away with a wage. Just enough to support a thin shell of dignity around them. Anytime he wanted to, someone could put his little finger through all the way into their lives. The farmers liked his father. They spoke seriously to him. They said he was a hard worker. When he said he wished someday he would be able to work for himself, that was the way he would say it, they would nod solemnly and tell him they thought it was a good idea. They approved. But then, they didn't know, on the other hand, even though the war had brought prices up, and there was no limit to the market, he was probably better off where he was. There was no telling when the war might end and it was an awful investment for a man, thousands of dollars for used machinery even to make a small start, and places were hard to get ahold of, some farmers were farming three or four places by themselves. The war effort. There were lots of ways to look at it. His father never said how he thought he'd get all that money.

Carl sat looking at the sky. Every time he killed anything, to eat it, to do it in that way, he was just doing their goddamn hackwork. Grow your own. Volunteer, when you're out of work. Isn't that it. A stupid willingness to be eternally used in that way. Has it got anything to do with the animals? How he felt about them had nothing to do with it. It's just disgusting use of myself, he said aloud.

Shortly after their arrival from the city, something went wrong with Mary's back. It pained her very much to walk or stand in one place for more than a few minutes. She had difficulty getting in and out of a car. She had gone to a doctor, but he had proposed removing her uterus and that seemed to both of them not funny at all. At least of questionable connection. They called him Dr. Quackman. However, he had been very helpful to them when they had first come. The eldest girl had had a high fever. The doctor arrived at the house late one afternoon at the end of his office hours. The house was empty, only the trunk they had brought and the sleeping sacks on the floor. The doctor was very much alarmed. Well, how can you live like this! he had demanded. Very brusquely and very professionally his eye had caught the abnormality of their arrangements. But, you don't even have a stove, he said. Why, you can't even cook. What do you do for a living, young man? Carl answered that he was just that week going up to the mountains to work in the woods. And in the meantime they had found this house and thought it best to move in even though they had nothing to do it with. Because they needed a house. The doctor examined the child and gave her a shot and all the while reflected on the strange place in which he found himself.

The doctor was a slightly pudgy man in his sixties, his hair very grey, but carefully groomed and wavy. He gave the impression of fastidiousness in his care for his body and his dress. For all that he looked somewhat seedy. In his businesslike manner he made them to understand that the next day he would send his wife around and she would see what she could do for them. She was interested in charities and indeed took an interest in people who were of the circumstances at hand. One very effective thing he did on that first visit was to tell the sick child she would have to go to the hospital if the shot did not prove enough. The prospect of this made such an impression on her that in a few hours she was well on her way to recovery.

The Wymans forgot all the foregoing as attributable to the eye of a man who lives well. Even though, as he stood by his white Cadillac convertible preparing to leave, he reminded them to expect his wife the next day. Shortly after noon she drove up, in another Cadillac, apparently her own. Through the window

Carl saw her arrive and was hesitant about going out to greet her. There was a fear in him of any more contacts that would draw attention to himself or his family because he was habitually suspicious of any efforts on the part of that sanguine body called society. It had not occurred to him then that the doctor considered them "interesting" people.

A large woman, full of energy, handsome, dressed in a tailored suit. She walked toward the back steps saying, So you're the people my husband told me about. My name is Gloria. Would you please carry in the things from the back seat? There are two big boxes of groceries. Gloria entered the house. Inside, they performed a little rite, explaining where they had come from, what their future plans were, and generally getting acquainted. Gloria was not the kind of person who ever got "chummy" with people like the Wymans, still she had an easy manner, vivacious and encouraging. Not that the Wymans tried to give her any hardluck story, but the very seeable difference in their way of living activated in them a slightly apologetic tone, and it was probably imagined by them that that tone, given the insecurity of their presence there, would make them less suspect people. But there seemed to be no element of suspicion in Gloria, and she continued talking about what might be done for them. She said, There is, as you probably don't know, an organization of women in this town called Women For Good and they just love to have someone like you people come around because generally the only people around here to help are Indians or Mexicans. Mary mentioned that although they might look as if they needed help, they had not arrived completely broke and the fact that Carl was going to work in the woods shortly should allow them to weather the next few days. Gloria replied by saying, Yes, I know what you mean, but your husband won't get paid right away if I understand how the logging work goes, and in the meantime you might be able to use any help you can get. Let me speak to the Women For Good because I'm sure they'd just jump at the chance to help. For instance they could get you a stove and some beds. What she said was perfectly reasonable. Mary and Carl ended by saying they would be willing to accept anything they needed. Gloria added that she thought Papa would have some spare mattresses and blankets in his clinic.

It was distasteful to Mary and Carl to accept furniture and the like not of their own choice. Still, an instant's reflection told them it would be weeks before they would be able to buy anything like tables and chairs and beds, let alone a stove. They had told themselves they could somehow manage by camping in the house. Perhaps. This arrangement, if there were anything to it, would make things easier, and if so, why not? They had never before been propositioned by charity, and found themselves a little curious about it. The Women For Good sounded as though it had some curious religious twist.

Gloria left in a cloud of wind and light dust, as she had arrived, as she would arrive anywhere, she was that kind of woman. The Wymans looked at the groceries. There was butter, and chickens. Steaks and a roast. There was a great meringue pie filled with banana cream. Gloria had brought an electric roaster along knowing they had no stove, and she had brought potato chips, explaining in a very detailed manner a nice way to fix chicken. Mary listened. You crush the potato chips and after dipping the chicken in melted butter you roll it in the chips and then bake it in the oven.

And she brought other boxes of food. Steaks and chicken, roasts and butter, creamy pies, elaborately frosted cakes, some with coconut. In other words she brought none of that plain food which is supposed to do the needy so much good.

Two Women For Good came to see into the business of a stove and other household things. There were things like knives and forks, plates and cups. They were neither jolly nor glum, and were in all ways willing to make the best estimate of what the family needed. When Mary told them she would like a wood cookstove, they protested at great length saying she would be smarter to have an electric one or at least bottled gas. But they finally capitulated, and after making a list, they departed saying some of the things would begin to arrive the very next day.

The following week Papa asked Carl if it would be all right if some things from the clinic could be stored in the barn. Carl thought this odd, that so prominent a man would need to call on them for storage space, but said of course. Put anything you want to in there. So the doctor brought a various collection of beds and mattresses and stools, in his pickup and his boys helped him carry it in through the narrow door. They occasionally saw Gloria around town driving in her car, always driving about, and she would wave and honk enthusiastically.

Now the child had fully recovered and Mary had gone to the doctor about her back and another of the children had a cold and was taken to him. Carl had been working in the woods for some time. Even the Women For Good had decided their support was no longer needed now that the family was more or less on its feet. After they had furnished the house with bare, but adequate, necessities, they too had brought food. There was a slight overlap in the charitable visits of Gloria and the Women For Good, but Gloria finally eased out of the situation with an expert diminishment of her attention and the other women assumed the full burden. The groceries brought by the Women For Good were plainer. Oleomargarine rather than butter, and no meat at all. They saw to it the family had food, and by this they meant "staples."

There came a time when the doctor had use for the things he had stored in the barn. He came with his pickup and sons. They were carrying a mattress. A sharp little nail sticking through the bottom of the door caught and made a long rip in it. The doctor looked up when he heard the rip—You clumsy fool, why don't you look what you're doing, why do you think I brought this stuff in here, to get it ripped, now look at that, the damn thing's ruined. Oh goddamit, you might as well put it on the truck but I don't think I can use it. You weak-headed idiot! The big dumb boy stood with his mouth half opened, a sort of disbelieving smile on his face. Another boy snickered, and the doctor frowned at him. Ya son of a bitch, the doctor said, and brushed his hands as he went back into the barn.

One sunny afternoon Mary walked downtown

to have her back examined. She waited in the outer
room and looked at some magazines and then was
ushered into an inner office. She lay on a table with
the back of her dress zipped down and finally the doc-
tor entered. He still thought her uterus should be
removed, so with this fixed idea in his head, his ex-
amination was perfunctory and quick. He prescribed
some pain relieving pills. She sat on a chair as she tied
her shoes. The back of her dress was still open. As he
was writing the prescription at his desk he suddenly
jumped up and ran his fingers through his hair. He
thought for a moment and said, Yes, yes, I forgot!
Whereupon he ran over and stuck his hand down the
loose front of her dress. He held her breast in his hand,
and stood there with apparently nothing else in mind.
They stared at each other for a brief moment. That's
all right! he said, and went back to writing the
prescription.

That was the last time Mary went to the house
in which Dr. Quackman had his offices, and it was the
last time either of the Wymans saw him except when
they noticed him driving along the street. Shortly after
that they saw the announcement of the opening of his
new clinic at the edge of town, on the road to Cedar
Mills. Mary mentioned to Carl the doctor's interest in
her breast. Carl said a bartender had told him that a
year ago Dr. Quackman's offices had been in the

Overton Building, that big burned out building on Main Street. The entire structure had been gutted and everything in it declared a total loss. He saved all that stuff, and figured to use it at his new place. And he collected insurance money for it! They were laughing. Of course, and our barn was the easiest place; certainly less unsightly than in with his saddles and blankets in his own barn.

THE UNEMPLOYMENT OFFICE

It was during the Fall sometime that Carl
FIRST MET BILLY HENDERSSON. CARL HAD FOR SOME
weeks gotten up bright and early in the morning and
gone to the unemployment agency, as it was known
by the workers. They did not use that appellation the
state prefers: employment office. This is one of those
truths that are so tested and tried by experience that
no amount of positive thinking can change it.

It was one of those days that appear in endless
number to those who look for work. Those days are
numb and temperatureless, their color a shade of dull
empty blue, and not grey as would seem the case. One
walks past the bank on the way and notices the smart
girls going in the back door to work, their dress, its

neatness, and sharpness, remains a very real impression. Their black shiny high heels click along the marble entryway, their hair kept from the wind by a gloved hand, their perfect teeth smile at the Bank Dick. A pleasant lingering mist of perfume stays on the air to remind one of their passing by. And so the tone of those days is set too, there is that smart clack of the heels. The breadman delivers his bread and the back of his truck is a banging signal to that early day security. But here the sense of it breaks up because there are always those signs to make the unemployed man happy, the breadman's job he would never want. He would take it perhaps, very likely he would, but he would never "stick to it," because he knows it is a terrible sort of job. Breadmen are born that way. They were destined to be breadmen, and there is no escaping the rigors of that destiny. The unemployed man has not been born to anything. At the same time that is his fate, it is also, never forget, his salvation. For practically no matter what is proposed for him to do he will do it, but money is the crux of his whole search, and he will never be misled by false propositions such as a "good, steady job" or a slogan such as "work your way up." No, there are two levels and two only in which money declares itself. The highest of course, is that in which there is such an amount that its "activity" is what makes money interesting, what it can do, like a toy train that can be switched, and made subject to elaborate signals. But then there is the level of the man who has none at all, and then the money he can get by whatever means takes on some qualities of this same operation. The smallest amounts, say two or three dollars, can suddenly become the levers with which he makes his little realm go. A cigarette, a glass of beer or wine, a loaf of bread, a little gas to go to the beach with, to dig clams, and yes, these men even buy a magazine then, but rarely a newspaper. What goes on in the newspaper is a step outside their world. But the point is that the money then becomes operative.

Money is not operative in the dim regions of those people who hold jobs as a matter of habit. One is not making any distinction like the middle class. This limb extends from the nightwatchman to the executive. It is a dim region in which the clashes and exchanges have had all their sounds removed, it is preordained. In some real sense it is still a vast area in which the most primitve bartering goes on, these people exchange their time and looks and attention or whatever it is they have, for a graduated scale of presence which in their more liberated moments they call their lives. In the uppermost world, as in the lowest, this would be an unthinkable contract.

It was Wednesday and Carl sat on a chair waiting. The inside of the state unemployment agency was familiar to him by this time. He felt at home there. There were several men he did not know but had learned to recognize and some of them now were talking acquaintances. An easy repartee establishes itself fairly soon in those circumstances, and a kind of dull humor enables one to exchange the rumors, usually without any substance whatever, about good paying jobs one place or another, and who you have to see and where you have to go, and so on. These men have long ago learned to suspect all this information either from the interviewers in the office or from among themselves, but it is a necessary and helpful pastime.

The walls are a sort of grey cream enamel, the color has stayed recognizable in a few spots where the light shines in through the metal venetian blinds on the windows. Many of the men are transients, some roll cigarettes, all look tired or if not that, absent-minded. Occasionally there is a bright kid walks in to take a "quick" check on the job situation and when he finds there is nothing, walks briskly out as if he would not deign to waste his time there, and as he goes he casts a quick disparaging look at the older men sitting in the rows of seats, waiting. Though none of them say it or even think it, they all know this child will learn either by becoming a breadman, or after a few more visits, he will take a seat too.

A quiet place. Most people understand what this

state institution is. As one is called to be interviewed he goes behind a counter or other barrier and takes a seat at the end of a desk facing the door. The interviewer a few years ago was dressed usually in a powder blue "suit" and had on a flowered necktie, and black shoes. Or if you set the same costume up in brown, he had on brown shoes. Thick, square pillars spaced evenly in rows held up the ceiling. The dress of the interviewer has changed a bit with the times, but the old interviewers sit there conforming to a late forties style of dress. The fact that the man seeking work sits facing the rear of the room has been carefully worked out, he is left by that arrangement with nowhere to go. It also is a basic policy of the state to give those on its side the first look at who enters a building.

A provocative scene was in progress at the counter. There was no loudness but one could feel by the tensions that all was not well. Carl noticed that one of the men had on the hat of a construction worker, what is called a hard hat, or a tin hat. This man's presence was cause for interest in itself. Either he was a logger or a construction worker, and in either case that was interesting because those two classes of workers would go into the unemployment agency only if their circumstances were critical. They had become accustomed to very high pay. Beside the man in the tin hat stood a smaller man, who looked very meek, and who needed a shave. He wore an old felt hat. They were talking with an interviewer.

The interviewer had just finished thumbing through some worn yellow file cards. He replaced them but kept one out. What do you mean? What's that got to do with it? Well, Mr. Hendersson, you see Mr. Willis here hasn't been in for a long time, he doesn't come around much, and you know, if he doesn't come around and stick with it, how can we judge how bad he needs a job. Anyway, as I've told you this is a slow season, I imagine when things break loose in the spring there might be something for him to do, but in the meantime I just don't know what to tell you. He hasn't got any trade, he can't do office work, he says he's never driven a truck. We just haven't got any straight labor work right now. You know yourself how slow that is, you're in the construction union. He's just not qualified. *Do you mean to tell me,* Mr. Hendersson began, that you have NO JOB WHATSOEVER FOR THIS MAN? YOU MEAN THERE'S NOT ONE JOB THIS MAN CAN DO IN THIS WHOLE BEAUTIFUL WEALTHY VALLEY HERE ON THIS SOUND? IS THAT WHAT YOU'RE TRYING TO SAY? Well, I don't know as I'd get that way about it, if I was you, Mr. Hendersson, the interviewer said, I could let him see one of the men at the desk, but after all this man has to take his own interest in things, I can understand that since he's your neighbor you feel something in the matter, but I'm not interviewing you. Do you want a job? NO! said Billy, I DON'T WANT ONE OF YOUR LOUSY SLAVEY JOBS, BUT THIS MAN'S KIDS ARE HUNGRY AND *HE* DOES. HAVE YOU EVER THOUGHT THAT NOT ALL OF HIS CALLS HERE HAVE BEEN RECORDED IN THIS SLOPPY SYSTEM, MOST OF THE TIME HE'S COME HERE TO WAIT AROUND TO GO HAYIN', ALL I WANT FROM YOU IS ONE STRAIGHT ANSWER—THETHERE IS NO JOB HERE THITHIS MAN CAN DO? RIGHT? It sounded as though Hendersson had a slight stutter.

The interviewer lit a cigarette. He put the lighter back in his pocket and blew the smoke out the side of his mouth and looked at the card again with his chin and his cigarette in the air. He went back to a bank of files. Mr. Hendersson and the little man stood and waited, watching. He returned with a sheet in his hand saying, No, it's about the only thing here, but it's not the right kind of a job for this man, in the first place you have to have a car to get there, and besides that, it doesn't pay enough. This man has twelve kids.

Hendersson's face had been red all along, it was probably naturally so, but on hearing what the interviewer had to say, it grew so fiercesomely red Carl thought the man's breath had failed. He stood staring at the interviewer for some moments, chewing on a toothpick. Suddenly he hit the counter with his fist and shouted, WHY YOU BASTARD! YOU'RE KIDDIN'! DOESN'T

PAY ENOUGH? WHAT THE HELL'S WRONG WITH YOU? THIS MAN NEEDS ANY MONEY HE CAN GET, TWO CENTS WOULD HELP HIM OUT RIGHT NOW . . . IF HE HAD TWO DOLLARS HE'D BE ABLE TO TAKE SOMETHING HOME FOR SUPPER. The interviewer was saying, Now wait, wait just a minute. WAIT HELL! HE'S BEEN WAITIN' ALL WINTER. LET ME SEE THAT JOB, and he reached for the card, I'LL TEAR THE SONOFABITCH UP! WHAT DO YOU MEAN HE HASN'T GOT A CAR! HE DOESN'T NEED ONE, CHRIST HE'LL WALK TO THE FUCKIN' JOB, HE'LL *CRAWL* TO IT. . . . WHAT KIND OF A MISERABLE GODDDDAMN JAJOB IS IT ANYWAY— POPOKING PEAS UPA AA RAT'S ASS? YOU MISERABLE BASTARD I OUGHTA THROW YOU OUT TH-THAT WINDOW!

By the time the interview closed Billy Hendersson was standing well away from the counter shaking his fist and several of the interviewers had advanced toward the front. The men in the agency sitting in the rows of chairs stared more alertly but for the most part just stared and held their breath. The interviewer had made some suggestion to a man at a desk over by the wall that the police be called. But suddenly Hendersson and the old man left. The room let out its breath as one and the only effect was the collection of interviewers standing in the back of the room, undistinguishable save for the two colors of their suits.

THE CONVERT

It was suggested to Carl by a righteous CITIZEN THAT IF HE REALLY WANTED WORK HE OUGHT to go from place to place asking for it, that the employment agency was not the place to find it. Carl did. He walked around several nearby towns for two weeks asking for work on the very spot, but when nothing came of this he returned to while away his mornings at the unemployment office. Sometimes there would be a farmer call in or drive up who wanted some work done. As he learned the system he would more frequently be there at the right moment. The work consisted of walking around and around, tramping silage as it was blown into the top of the silo. The work was as uneventful and regular as that of a horse pulling

a pole around a gear exchange to elevate ears of corn.
The silos were on dairy farms which grew silage to feed
their herds during the winter. There was nothing to
it, you simply got in the silo when it was empty, and
walked your way up, as it filled. Walking. That was
all. At noon the men inside, usually three, climbed
down the ladder on the outside, going through one of
a series of holes which, as the silage piled higher, was
plugged up with a wooden door.

There was one man who always wore a black
welder's cap. He and Carl worked together often. His
name was Blackie. He had a clubfoot and his whole
life consisted, as far as Carl could tell, of tramping
down silage and sitting in the Baseball Tavern drinking
beer. He said very little except when lunch was called,
at which time he became animated, always saying
something very irrelevant like, It's a pretty nice day ain't
it. And he smiled. Carl was disturbed by the severity
of his limp and thought that of all work the man could
be doing this was the worst. But Blackie was a figure
who stood alone. Inside the farmer's house he ate like
a man mad. He was so concentrated in his eating that
it was a joke on the part of his fellow workers. Winos
have a quiet serenity when they are eating; they have
not had anything to eat for days perhaps, and at noon
after they have done work that has been hard on them,
given their condition, they eat as though it were a gift.

A strange politeness prevails as they sit at the table, all washed, unshaved, quiet.

After a time Carl was hired by two brothers who had an outfit of trucks and grass harvesting equipment. He drove a truck for them. The only men left in the silo were the exhausted winos, tramping all day long, packing down the silage. Every now and then Blackie would be on the silo crew where Carl was hauling from the fields. They would wave to one another. And if Blackie had climbed down for a drink of water, they talked. The days were mostly sunny and Carl enjoyed being in the fields. Barn swallows swept over the newly cut grass, feeding in the air. Brewer blackbirds were on the ground in great numbers picking seeds. Single crows lumbered up off the ground as the truck approached. Killdeer ran along the fence rows their heads bobbing. A plaintive and penetrating cry.

But that season ended and Carl was back again on the chairs of the office. Since he was a familiar figure around there by that time, the interviewers recognized him and one day asked him if he would work on a chicken farm. The farmer's name was Albert Wonder. His place was about five miles out of town. The work consisted of gathering eggs, cleaning out from under the roosts, and filling the trays with feed. Al was a tall, lean, handsome man who had

been a hellraiser in his youth but after he had met his
wife and married, he got religion and was very much
a Hell and Brimstone quoter of the Bible. It was all
Grace. The church he had joined, an evangelical
church, discouraged reading in the Old Testament.
He was an easy man to get along with and Carl
enjoyed the work. It was somewhat steady and the
pay was fair. Carl took his midday meal with the
Wonders, that was part of the day. When Al was not
quoting the Bible apropos of nothing, he was
remembering with a dreamy look in his eye the days
when he had a motorcycle. But those were evil,
indulgent days, a man hasta get that out of his
system, he would add, with his jaw set. Even so
excellent a man as Peter, didn't he deny Christ three
times? And then he would say, If that's so, an
ordinary man will suffer many errors and take many
wrong turnings, his mistakes will be manifest. Why,
all those women I used to jump into bed with in the
days I had my motorcycle, that was evil. It was. It
was the most sinful, the most rotten thing a man ever
did. And a gleam of fond remembrance would enter
his eye.

   Al mixed his own feed and these one way
lectures to Carl usually took place in the feed room
but they could occur anywhere, like cleaning the
roosts, or when they met in the doorway of one of the

laying rooms. Carl at times felt guilty that he was not earning his pay because Al took so much of the time talking of God and Jesus. Al demanded full attention. Until he got used to the smell of the chicken house, Carl would nearly faint waiting for this evangelist to be done. At the first chance he rushed out into the cold air, sweating from the heat of the hen house, to deliver his eggs to Al's wife who ran the cleaning machinery in the egg room. She was more stout than fat and not so tall as Al, but had more authority in the long run and was not quite such a revivalist. She worried less about Carl's soul than she did the gathering of the eggs on time. She looked with a wary eye on these small impromptu revival meetings. So did Carl, but for a different reason—he was getting a little obsessed with Christ. Up to the time he started working with Al his feelings along that line had been casual. Part of Al's pitch was of course patently nervousness as when he would say, Before the Lord showed me the true path I smoked too, like you do and I drank too, of course you've said you aren't a drunkard, oh truly I was and I chased women, and do you know when Brother Chastus took me in that night I could feel the wonderful warm feeling of the Lord come over me by degrees and I was still in sin because I couldn't believe it, still in sin, but it was a sin that was being fought over in a great death struggle waged between the Devil and the Lord. And the Lord won, oh yes He did, I saw Him do it.

The conversations at the dinner table were made of desultory light gossip. Carolyn Wonder served huge starchy meals. There were four of them at the table, the Wonders' youngest son, Jackie, had not yet started to school. The boy was a very messy eater, sometimes he would throw his fork into the mashed potatoes or he might take his soup, which he did not like, and mix it with the macaroni. If Al that morning had been especially successful with his candidate he would ignore this with a beatific smile and say, Jackie, look what you did now, and then muss up the boy's hair with a hand. But if the reverse were true, and some large bills from the co-op had come in the mail, he might smack him so soundly with the back of his hand the boy would go sprawling over by the stove. Carl would wince and look out the window. And there was Jackie—his chair, his plate, and himself, on the floor, screaming like a siren clogged with mashed potatoes. Carl would sometimes find he had lit a cigarette as the Blessing began. Carolyn might start the conversation by saying, Didgew know Georgia Baxter is having another one? Jackie, the classical snotty-nosed brat would then fling a piece of food with his fork. Carolyn would slap him smack on the nose. Three minutes of uninterrupted screaming with his mouth so wide open his eyes were invisible. Al would look at Carl and say, You should of been there last night, Mrs. Baxter spoke in tongues. Then he would lay his fork down with a slight roll to his eyes, and continue, It was the most beautiful thing you could ever see. Hilda Anderson was there and she said it was the purest Swedish she'd ever heard and do you know, Mrs. Baxter can't speak a word of Swedish! Isn't that amazing, Carl would say.

There was a puerile curl to Al's lip although he had rather a handsome face. Carl would at times speculate to himself over the possibilities of a downfall, or a backsliding, in Al's case. That women still troubled him there was no doubt. The few times the Wyman family had been over to the farm together for supper, Al had definitely given Mary an appreciative eye. Once Mary caught him, as she was to speak of it later. After that Al gave her a very righteous eye, and Mary was under the burden of being made to think she had tempted him. She was always after that a little uncomfortable, and amused, in his presence.

So it went. Carl did not mind the work. Most of the time he rather enjoyed it. He wandered around through the rooms of the chicken houses gathering eggs and filling the hoppers with feed. He worked mostly by himself. The old rooms were soft and dark, filled with a dusty light. In these rooms there was a one foot layer of sawdust on the floors, it was marked with depressions where the hens had dusted. The smell of ammonia was faint and pleasant. The hens laid their eggs in straw nests, warm and soft to the hand. In the rooms upstairs in the big barn Wonder had installed the first of his automatic machinery. The feed was carried along a continuous belt between the hung wire cages. The smell was very strong, the droppings piled up on the floor beneath raw and wet. The eggs rolled out of the cages into a tray. The chickens were all tranquilized in that room. Into their feed was mixed various drugs, to calm them, to alert them, to saturate them with protein. After seven or eight months of intensive laying they were burnt out. By the time they were sold for meat they looked five years old. And the cannibalism was terrific. There were three or four chickens in each cage. If one of them got the slightest eruption on its skin or comb the others smelled it and ate the sick chicken's life away if it was not rescued in time. To reduce the can- nibalism, their beaks had to be burned off with a hot clamp; they looked like old people with puckered mouths. They were susceptible to the same mass

neuroses that develop in a housing project or a high
rise or in suburbia. Wonder spent much of his time
going through those cages checking for hens that were
not laying, for growths and malignancies, for the
blind and crippled. He could spot those with enlarged
livers by the look of the comb, color of the legs and
feet. Those that staggered or seemed to have erratic
and wandering attentions suffered from nervous dis-
eases. All these he culled. It was an endless process.
Often he sought Carl out and took him along on those
culling excursions. Al would remember almost
exactly the cage or room from which he had heard a
crow when he was carrying feed. Carl asked how a
rooster got in there. It ain't a rooster, it's what they
call a sex reversal. It happens all the time in chickens
according to a government pamphlet I read. You see,
a hen is born with a good left ovary but the right one
is little and undeveloped, if something happens to the
left ovary, the right one gets to be a gonad and the hen
starts to crow and develop a big comb. While he
preached to Carl of the virtues and trials of Paul he
performed on-the-spot autopsies with his pocket
knife. He had a quick deft way, with his thumb and
index finger, of breaking the neck and then holding it
until spasms died away and then he would make an
incision in the area of the part he wanted to inspect.
You see? The kidney is corrupt! Or if it were the liver

• 95

he brought out with his fingers he would hold it in the palm of his hand and give Carl a significant look. Then he would turn the dry ocherish thing over and say, You see? It has become vile. It is vile. Vile. It has succumbed to vileness. This strongly biblical analysis of the chicken's troubles hardly failed to amuse Carl, but at the same time it made him uneasy. It made him uneasy because he could never precisely determine what was on Al Wonder's mind. What it was made him so intense about love, Brotherly Love to be sure, because if not in practice, in discussion every other kind of love was carnal. But Wonder would confuse him at times by joking about the blindness and bigotry of religious people. He was as exclusive as any Catholic about the possibilities of redemption for those people not of his church. And standing by the cages dissecting chickens he would divide Carl's attention between the pragmatic matter of the immediate illness and the theoretical illnesses of the world, with that sign of the true American Fundamentalist on his face, an infinitely superior beatitude. Each exhibition of a sick gall bladder, each laying open of a crop, brought his expression back to the business at hand, a look of blank interest, his overly youngish mouth hanging slightly open as he applied the criteria of his trade to the troubled part.

Sometimes during those sessions Carl grew

melancholy. He thought he should not be there for some reason he could not fathom. He would brood, half listening to Wonder expound an Epistle of Paul, a hen throbbing on the edge of death in his hands. He would brood on how he came to be there and how he could get away . . . he didn't have to do this work, there were all those other short-term jobs. It made him uncomfortable that Al assigned the work for the day, and then, at nine-thirty or ten in the morning caught him in the entry way of a laying room to talk until noon. And at noon they stayed in the house often until two-thirty or three. He figured Wonder knew what he was doing, he wouldn't argue with it. He was being paid. But the chickens had to be taken care of and that meant he must stay on in the evening finishing up the chores. Most every night he arrived home after dark. It was getting worse. But he knew very well why he continued to work for Albert Wonder. It was a relief to have some steady money. Such a simple matter as Mary being able to buy easily prepared food. An operation on her spine had cured the trouble with her back but it would be a long time before she was strong again and Carl could not let her go back to those long hot hours over the wood stove trying to invent a meal from cheap, bulky food.

Still, a way out of it was always on his mind. He told himself that it was something innate in him, he couldn't stick to anything. He asked himself why he fought against this job, he wasn't doing anything else now and didn't have anything in mind to do, so why not settle into it knowing what it was, give himself a fixed date, then quit. It was much better than scuffling days on end at the unemployment agency.

But he missed seeing his friends, and the transients, he missed the abstract urgency of their talk. The sidewise way they had of bringing up the most trivial issue, like how many miles away a town was, and endlessly tilting information until, no matter how plain, it had been made to show all its surfaces. Hey, you're smoking Dukes Mixture, let's see the label. Yes I did hear that was named after Doris Duke, but I doubt if she smokes it. She might, she might, might roll 'er own, there're some weird people, wear old cloths just like bums, fuck around in all sort of places you wouldn't expect 'em to. You wouldn't even know they were there. Well you sure as hell wouldn't, every time I ever see you you got your eye on the sidewalk lookin for butts. Ya, well I wasn't lookin for your goddamn clapped-up butt! I been keepin an eye out for Doris Duke's butt. Well I'll be damned, you think she ain't got clap? Maybe, maybe. If she has she got it someplace they sure as hell wouldn't let you in, Christ! They'd throw your ass out of a place like that so fast what little brains you got left would arrive tomorrow on the slow freight, the conductor'd throw 'em off with his sandwich wrappers, shit! The depot flunky'd be out there with his broom and dustpan sweepin' that mess up before you uncrossed your eyes and took your finger outa your ass. Well—you talk with such experience that must be the story of how *you* lost your fuckin' mind!

Yes, the endless coprolalia, he missed that. The wild accuracy of that foul, vented speech. And the sturdiness of their resignations; it had a quieting effect on him because there was a deadly sophistication about it, he thought of them as pure scientists inspecting their own isolated condition. It was a ritual for them to explain to themselves with an antiseptic sense of duty every one of the reasons they should not accept a job just offered before they took it. A protective magic. You know, we're gonna get out there and that bastard's not gonna be ready to start whatever pissy-assed little chore he wants us to do, and you *know* he's not gonna pay until the minute we start, and when he does he's gonna give us some phony personal check he wrote out with a stubby little pencil he licked he looks that stingy, and they ain't gonna wanta cash it at the Baseball, unless you're lucky enough to have a tab to pay off then they'll take it even if it's bad those greedy sonsabitches. And if you don't bust your ass on this one you ain't gonna be *invited* back, yeah, that's a good one, no you ain't gonna be *invited* back to bust your ass tomorrow. I can see his dumpy wife now killin' a cull chicken or two to feed us poor hard workin' men and feeling so good about it when we eat like refugees. Oh bullshit! Let's climb into his shiny red pickup truck, careful there now don't step on the spare tire . . . hey I wonder if he'd miss that sonofabitch? Yeah, that's right, he's got it wired for burglars.

Once in a while there was a day off during the week. Al would be in town all day and do the feeding at night by himself. Carl heard the union was taking in new members for the oil refinery going up near Anacortes. Even so, the union was hard to get into, there were a lot of men out of work. The only thing to do was hang around the union hall. He went in wherever he could.

The leaves were nearly gone from the scattering of alders in the valley. Carl could not bring himself to tell Al about the union. He felt that he ought to feel some obligation to the Wonders. Not beholden, he never felt exactly that way. It was difficult. The relationship had turned into something he could not have expected. Now when he drove up in the morning, if Al was outside and saw him there came the smile and the talk right off of the great advantages of getting with Jesus. Al wanted to save a soul. He was getting serious about it. It had been possible for Carl to get him off onto other subjects, his friend in the asylum who was put there by his Catholic mother, stories of his hell-raising youth, his evil experiences with women. Al liked very much to recall those days. But it was getting more and more difficult for Carl to turn the conversation in that direction.

The strange mixture in Al of the practical, aspiring businessman and the evangelist, and how he could talk on for hours inside those loud contradictions. It amused Carl, and sometimes irritated him, that Al could assume such wisdom in the detailed consideration of what was wrong with Carl's way of life. One day, with some avid plagiarism of the Sermon on the Mount, Al told Carl that his loyalties were divided, he could not serve two masters at the same time, he had to choose, and in the end, when this show is up, it's going to be one way or the other and the man who loved *this* life is going to find out to his great dismay that the jig's up, that's all she wrote, all transitory, and what good is fornicating after all but the silliest smallest briefest little pleasure, a pleasure turned into an everlasting pain to be paid off forever, more than the unjustest debt any man around here could demand, a debt of pain unknown but to be believed, oh yes, you must believe it! And do you know, he looked Carl in the eye, Do you know the one little thing you have to do to make it all right? Humble yourself to Jesus, to God! man, just humble yourself that's all, that's *all*. Ask and it shall be given you! Just knock, and it shall be opened unto you. That's all in the world you have to do.

But I've told you, Carl said, I like Christ very much, I can say I love him. He is one of the best men I ever heard of, I've told you that Al, I always thought so, from Sunday school class on. I can hardly disagree with you, but I don't know what you want. I've told you I think you live in a self-deceiving world, you run this farm like anyone else would run it, and then you preach all this renunciation of life on earth that you read about in the New Testament, you support usury every day with those loans you have to have to keep going and Jesus put that use of money down, why don't you walk into the First National Bank and kick the president's ass out? Those very bums you go down to the jail to preach to on Sunday afternoon are better than you, they neither sow and they sure as hell don't reap, except for the people who'd have them shot after their use is over, but you'd call that loving thine enemy? Maybe they do pay attention to that one verse of Matthew though—agree with thine adversary quickly lest at any time the adversary deliver thee to the judge and the judge deliver thee to the officer, and thou be cast in prison. I mean they try to keep that in mind most of the time because for them it's pretty good advice. It saves a lotta busted heads and they are generally the kind of people who have so *little* at stake in *This World* it isn't worth getting their brains jarred. Yeah, that's practical. And you'll say it has nothing to do with salvation.

Carl stopped talking and thought again Al's strictness on that point was rather admirable no matter how at times it disgusted him. Al was putting feed in the mixer. He was smiling. Watching him, Carl thought the Church of God did give Al something. It gave him something abstract to think about. The bank would never do that. Those bills for fifteen hundred dollars from the feed company were not abstract. And Al was a Good Man. He had been specific about it. When Mary came home from the hospital Al helped him put hot water in the house for her, something Carl could never have done by himself. Al knew many trades—welding, plumbing, carpentry, he could fix cars and tractors. Al enjoyed being at their place, they sat around drinking coffee and talking when they were not working and then Al never brought up religion. Both Mary and Carl joked about Al's undeniable interest in Mary. The old lust in his eye. It seemed very respectable. His religion had not dominated him in any basic way. It had come to him late, just a year or so before Carl knew him, and Al was still young. Carl thought perhaps those people who "get" religion, as a fresh force, rather than having it as a dead, set factor of their genes, are sometimes better off. Al Wonder took an interest in Carl's books that was neither polite nor real. The very idea of books bored him. He looked at all of them as naturally less than the Bible, as just another set of objects in the outer world. He liked to read the Bible, and only two or three books of that, because he liked to think of himself as doing it. Finally he most liked to *hear* the preacher. He liked what was aurally fantastic. Carl did not discover this until too late. Al's interest in religion was secondary, he used the energy of the interest to keep himself straight, like an alcoholic who must repeat constantly that drink is the agent of his doom. Not drink but the fast life of sex was the spectre Al challenged. A man otherwise conventional in every way but marked by a single and definite sign.

Al picked up a book and stared at Mary. She could not stand it directly, and she had told Carl so, and told him she thought Al was attractive in a way no other man had been to her before, but it was all a strange fascination, she didn't feel any plainly sexual impulse toward him. She reasoned with herself when she spoke of it. It wasn't a fear, she thought, although she couldn't be sure, and therefore it might have something to do with "fornication," and she had laughed at that word she wasn't interested to admit or recognize. In any case she was willing to put it down as a puzzle. But when Al talked to her directly she usually ended by lowering her eyes no matter how hard she tried not to. Carl saw the book he was thumbing through was *Moses and Monotheism*. When Al consciously tried to avoid religion, when his common sense told him it was out of place, he used Love as an alternative admonishment. He said to Mary, You know, Moses was full of love, *that's* why he was a great leader. He sure as hell was, Carl thought, looking through the smoke of his cigarette at Al. Just like Brigham Young, young as you can get 'em, a traveling harem whooping across the mountains and the plains, yas chillun, we's headed for the promised land, Here! It! Is! Now all you girls under fifteen and a half lay down on your backs and throw them legs apart and we'll celebrate this here little occasion on the spot, careful now! don't crowd each other there's plenty of room on the prairie, stand back, spread out, Hey, you old women, keep your shoulders on them carts, there's a long way to go before supper, move along now! distance is fooling in the mountains, that's right, move along! you don't need to pay attention to what's going on here, this here is a ritual, we're all saints here, keepa goin' . . .

Yes, Al said, He loved his brothers and sisters and he brought them all back home. Al looked long and closely into Mary's eyes, looking at her as though he were trying to think, but Carl asked himself, Just how literally does he mean that? Al put his hand on Mary's knee, You know, that's all any spiritual leader is, any great man, a man who feels love in his heart, not lust, not the unredeemable filth of fornication we find here on earth, not the covetousness, those desires we have to guard against every minute we're awake. Oh God! Carl thought, The laying-on-of-hands.

Was Moses really a lover, Carl asked, or was he the first lawyer, you know Jesus had to make the point that if you *thought* about committing adultery, with someone in mind, that was the same thing as *committing* it. I always thought Jesus was more interested in making that clear than in putting adultery down. Al took his hand away and looked at Carl with great interest. That's right! That's right. That is right. But now you're forgetting what it was I told you—the New Testament is Grace, and the Old Testament is Judgement. "But I say unto you love your enemies, bless them that curse you," is the bringing of love

106 •

into *us* . . . The Old Testament is vengeful. That night Carl walked with him out to his car and Al told him it was a shame he had waited so long before arranging for Mary to have hot water.

Carl stood leaning against the mixer while Al dumped the various sacks of oats, wheat, barley, ground corn, dried green grass he called greens, and the chemicals he called concentrates into the hopper. Amphetamines and sulfa compounds. A long thin window of lucite allowed one to see the ingredients being whirled about inside. The machine hummed.

The chicken farm stood well up on the gentle slope of a hill. Through the window in the feed room Carl could see the valley spread out below, running its jagged course west toward the Sound. Each farm in that valley had some alder and larch, filled with grey light, among the always present dark green, the impenetrableness, of the fir and hemlock. The darkened and worn red of the barns.

In the orchard the winter apples hung bright red and fixed against the green fabric of the woodlot. Beyond the orchard, pullets ran, white trajectories through the solar space of the brilliant uncorrupted apples. The leafless boughs of winter apples, turned by frost to gold. Those chickens are almost old

enough to be moved inside, thought Carl as he heard
Al start talking again, the eggs they lay are getting
larger. A sudden breeze filled his window view with
leaves.

Carl continued to stare at the window. He
listened to Al with an unengaged, obscure part of his
mind. Completely without resentment Al smiled and
laughed as he told the story Carl had heard many
times, how the preacher, Brother Chastus, had taken
the glorious light of God to the natives of Haiti. Carl
felt dead from some kind of supreme bewilderment,
his whole concentration was out the window. He
thought the only life left in him was in his eyes, and
his eyes were on the window and the window was an
extension of his own eyes, a direct part of him, the
only instrument he had in that instant to transport
himself. He felt weak, his body felt numb and larger
than normal. His own physical presence seemed
autonomous. Separate. Then he saw a man in the or-
chard and all this displacement froze in him. It hung
in the trees a flat spectre with long auburn hair, he
held a staff. He was dressed in farmer's overalls and
a straw hat, a lamb stuck in the air, in the branches
beside him. Carl shut his eyes. He felt impossibly op-
pressed, and so tired he could not stand up, he sat
back on a sack of grain. His hand was over his
mouth. Tears were slowly filling his eyes. He was

overcome. He would never be the same again.

But you're wrong about those men in jail, he heard Al say, I love them like brothers, the deepest sinners are the most precious gifts we can bring to the Lord. Al took up a large scoopful of terramycin and threw it into the hopper. The mixing was done.

He's burning up the bones of the chickens, forcing the eggs from them, prying them out with chemical levers, Carl thought. Love. Love, love. He sat on the sack completely tired and completely bored. He wanted to see Mary. Be at home, shut away. He was not amused anymore. He could not sit in Al's livingroom again and watch the Oral Roberts program where the cripples threw away their walking sticks, the blind men removed their dark glasses while Al cheered and pounded the divan because his team was winning. The sun was falling. Carolyn walked into the feed room and shouted, Good God! Haven't you guys even *started* to feed the chickens yet?

They picked up the buckets and filled them with the mixed feed and then entered separate rooms to fill the hoppers. Carl was sad, and felt it a relief to do the work. He liked both of them but he knew when he got in his car this evening and drove off he would never be back. Every few minutes he would meet Al on his way back to the feed room; they spoke briefly while they stood at the mixer waiting for the buckets to fill. The sound of Carolyn's voice came up from the house when she called the children in to wash for supper. The air of the valley took on a bluish cast as the light failed.

The Difference

Mary tried to recall whether or not she
HAD EVER OFFERED THE USE OF THE BATHTUB TO
Ramona. She decided hopefully she had. She said later
she could almost see Ramona coming out of the
bathroom drying herself saying it was wonderful. The
ease of it, the casual and completely unthought
convenience. It might have been the one thing Ramona
wholly admired about civilization. She had come from
a harsh climate into a different but still harsh climate
and a bathroom seemed more than any other apparatus
to allow her to make the adjustment from a primitive
past to a still primitive present. Certainly the English
language hadn't helped. To have learned to read and
write had not. She would always be an Esquimau to

those skills. To flush a toilet in harsh weather, or to take a bath in a private bathroom was an advance. The outhouse at the camp was without a roof and until they got an umbrella, Ramona had gone out with a newspaper on her head in the everlasting northwest rain, shielding her head as she sat. After they got the umbrella she took that, and it was a great improvement.

There were many things that unsettled the Wymans in their relations with the McCartys. The bathtub was not that important, really.

Ramona never complained about anything except the toilet. There was one time Mary had given a blouse to Ramona, she had made it out of some silk her brother brought back from Japan during the war. It was old but still very nice stuff. Ramona was shy about taking it; Mary was not for some time able to tell why. Finally Ramona said she couldn't use it because it was so sheer and she had no slip to wear under it.

James spoke his words with the same subtle deformity his body took. When he got drunk they were more clipped and rapid, and he sometimes made a hissing noise with his mouth. He was often finished speaking before one expected it. He had a way of throwing back his head and laughing, his cap slipped around to the side, the bill sticking up over his ear.

His drunkenness was compelling then. At other times he could be mean, as if some dark impatience controlled him. Once the Wymans went downtown to do some shopping with Ramona, they stopped on the way to get a beer and were not back home as soon as they had expected. Waiting for their return, James stumbled about the house slapping Davie and shoving the bottle into his mouth saying, Here drink this damn you. The Wyman children, especially the eldest, John, were frightened by the baby's crying and the gyrations of the drunken man.

When Ramona was drunk she was very very inarticulate and would stagger around the room mumbling beneath her breath. She was always so gentle she never frightened the children. Yet her northern intensity seemed dangerous. She would wait for five minutes, staring with squinted eyes, to finally reply, Sheeeit, and then flick the ashes of her cigarette on the floor. And then very softly, You don't know what you're talking about. You haven't been there. What do you know. Uh huh . . . sure . . . You've lived, you have . . . Uhmmm . . . squinting intensely. Well! a bright smile would appear as if she had awakened. Well, what do you say, this is pretty nice isn't it . . . Yes, this is pretty nice. Yes, this is pretty nice. Oh yes, uh HUH. James! What the hell do you mean: leave that kid alone. Leave him. Leave him.

• 113

Come on James! Oh shut up, Ramona! you don't know what you're talking about. All you can do is get into bed with all those guys. Guys, Ramona! That's all you know. That's the difference. You don't know. You don't know, Ramona! That's it! That's what you do! And Ramona would say, Oh, Carl's right. Carl's right. You ought to stop drinking long enough to get your tools. That's it, you bastard, you're not going to work, you never will.

But that was not quite true. James would have gone to work. It was true in the sense that he did not go to work. Certainly. But when work was offered him he did work. Without hesitation. It was rarely work that would improve the McCarty family. Work that improves one is hard indeed to come by. So he was for the moment stuck with the Farmer Smith. Smith it was who owned the pea camp and he needed a handy man. James lapsed into that man. He fixed windows, and roofs and the sides of buildings and he ran errands too, be sure. It was what Carl had done on the chicken farm, adjusted by the use of a trade, and that adjustment was small.

Of course Smith was not Wonder. Wonder was a man, no matter what his propensities for a certain provocation of the spirit, who did indeed struggle in his way against the same elements anyone else does. He had his insurmountable debts, he had his directives from the agriculture department. That kind of circle is endless. Smith, on the other hand, had come by, one way or another, several sections of rich flat land and he needed to borrow from no one. He was undistracted by religion—Christ could climb on a tractor and plough for all he cared. It would be by the hour in any case. He had not a farm but many farms. He was a humorless man who saw that life was simple and all to his purpose and the main thing he did besides get into his car and go to town was to oversee his fields of strawberries and grass. He had no close touch with those he worked. In the busy seasons the men and women and children under him numbered in the many scores, and during the short winter he still kept about him twenty or thirty retainers. Some, like James, performed skilled work at a rate only a down-and-out man would be happy to receive. Smith's house, east of town, was an enigma of stone facade and enormous hip roofs and the applied skills of science. Thermopanes. When his pickup truck flew around his fields, which was an affectation in itself, his workers looked up to see his coming in awe.

When the rain failed in that land of perpetual rain, Smith drilled an easy well for aerial irrigation, and if that well failed he charged it to the government, his enjoyment of such leniency the government makes to large farmers in distress was complete. And in

the worst of seasons this same man who enjoys that
government which makes for him a private little
welfare state, sees fit to tolerate a group of tortured
and beaten men who have nowhere else to go. His
"generosity" is all the more amazing because the
nature of strawberries and peas and sweet corn and
such seeds as cauliflower and beet, and cabbage,
requires the constant presence of a few men. Those
who come in season have spent the winter in
California, Arizona, and southern Texas. They
return in the spring smiling, warmed by the winter
sun. In the little shacks they will shift for themselves.
There will be newly married sons and daughters
crammed in with the still expanding families of the
old folks. There will be the few Indians who have
stayed close to the northern border. There is always
a grandmother with them, the hanging-on old
grandmothers the Indians seem to insist on carrying
around. She who will probably smoke a cigarette
when she can get it. The last witness of a culture.

Sometimes James needled Carl. Usually about the
day work Carl was doing, or about why the Wymans
were in that part of the country anyhow. He may
have felt in some vague way that the Wymans were

"slumming" and at times expressed resentment. What the hell are you doing here—you're wasting your time, you can't get anything out of this! Why hell! You have to be a great man to see things, look at Spinoza. He didn't come to a burg like this, hell, no! He went places. You have to have something on the ball, you can't be around and be a second-rater. Second-rate never got anybody anyplace. And then he would let his head drop. James sometimes talked of his past. His half brother who lived in this same valley was a dunce, by James' bitter estimation, but he could never quite discount the fact that this half brother had a good job making lots of money as a surveyor. James had been the black sheep of the family. He remembered very well traveling in an Auburn in the early thirties. Up the coast through Oregon and Washington to Vancouver Island. His family had a cabin then near Oyster River. He said, One time we stopped in a little town in Oregon and my mother went into a drugstore. She came back out and we started off, we had a Phaeton, the top came down you know, and our little brother climbed up on the back seat and jumped out. We were just little kids and didn't say anything about it for about three miles. Boy, was Mom mad. Wasn't that something? Imagine that, Jesus, you can't just lose a kid in the middle of nowhere, they won't allow it!

James was born in Hollywood. He would say, You never heard of that did you? Nobody comes from there. When we were kids we used to ride around in convertibles and reach up and pick avocados off the trees right from the street. Those old women used to come screamin' out of their houses, wow! And then he would take a drink of beer, taking the bottle up in his crooked hand in a little short motion ending in what always seemed a very short drink. Then he would gaze off. Thinking of something else. His eyes were as grey as his cap, and his legs always crossed. He sat in a chair rocking a crossed leg. Ramona would say quietly, Sheeit!

There were those times the Wymans were doubtful that they could put up with all the drinking. And then Carl would say to Mary, I like these people very much, there aren't many people one can talk to around here, but it gets too much. The hours get so late and they never go. Mary would nod. And say, Yes, but what are they going to do. James has been looking for a job for a long time, and they've been looking for a house, they can't seem to connect with anything. I don't know what to say. Ramona seems so damn decent and human and is an awfully conventional woman, Carl. Finally, she wants all the things everyone wants. Toilets and groceries, and bathtubs, she wants a husband who is not any better than

James, but who can somehow get a job. She wants curtains on her windows and she wants windows. Have you ever thought of that? She wants windows. After all, when she was a school teacher no matter how much a native she still was, she learned to think of herself as different. We know that's absurd, and so does she really, but how can you be impatient with such a thing? Good God, I can't stand it when they come here and slop around, but the world's even more distasteful from the other side. Much more. Do you ever think that those friends of yours in the City would get t.b. They never would! They'd cover their mouths with handkerchiefs if they passed someone like Ramona. They are so cognizant they would know right off about an Esquimau anyway. Talk about not taking chances! And have you ever thought that those people have constructed a very damned unalterable determination to live. Good God, they cling to life as though it were precious when all their experience, not violent, or *interesting* at all, but dull, and uniform, and subtle, tells them it's cheap.

New Year's Eve

In the town there were four taverns. MARMOT'S TAVERN WAS PATRONIZED BY MEXICANS, Indians, and Construction Workers. Drurer's Tavern was primarily for farmers. The WhileAway was a triangular shaped building conforming to the cut against the grid the railroad made. The WhileAway had for its regular clientele pensioners, old men pensioned from one place or another, who sat in the back room playing cards all day long. Halfway between Marmot's and the WhileAway, was The Savoy. This tavern, unlike the other three, did not have a peculiar clientele, it drew on all the population. Since it was a spill-over, a place to stop on the way to the other taverns, its business thrived. There it was not unusual to see

Esquimaux, Indians, businessmen, loggers, construction workers, farmers, Mexicans, tramps. All four taverns were on the main street.

The towns in the lower valley are close together, some not more than five miles apart. They are separated by four miles of dwindling countryside, the black green hemlocks stand singly or in small groves along the highway.

New Year's Eve Carl took Mary downtown for a glass of beer. They went first to The Savoy. There was a mixture of snow and rain outside and as they went through the door Mary took off her black beret and hit it against her skirt. She was wearing an orange coat with a large black imitation fur collar. They sat at the bar. Toward the back of the room was one large booth. Along one wall, opposite the bar, was a line of regular booths. The woman who owned The Savoy hired a man bartender who ordinarily worked a shifting schedule with her, but tonight they were both in attendance. The woman was hard, washed-out and Klondike looking. Her cheeks were brightly daubed with rouge, and her lips wore a thick covering of heavy red. She had a high metal laugh and short-changed the customers when, in her judgement, they were drunk enough. She exuded such an air of heavy sweet perfume one felt its tendrils out on the sidewalk when merely passing by. Inside the tavern the odor was so strong it sometimes gave the initiate pause, a new drinker in that place could be observed to glance around suspiciously. Her smile, and she smiled often, was not really unpleasant, but was alarming, her teeth were large and yellow. Be that as it may, her laugh was pleasant, and though she was well past the age of desirability, she possessed a certain loud attractiveness.

Mary turned once to find herself being stared at by the man on the next stool. He wore a green tweed cap and was dressed in the green wool of a logger come to town. He had a round face and a sharp nose. He said, You're Canadian. She replied, No, I'm not. Mary did not like the way he looked at her. The man said nothing more for a while. The place was noisy. Then he said, Well what *are* you? Well, I'm what I look like I am, whatever that is, she said. If you mean where am I from, I'm from here in town. He laughed and took a drink of his beer and looked down the bar toward the door. People came and went, of course. Among those who came in was Leonard with his short, pudgy wife. He put a hand on Carl's shoulder and smiled as he went by.

The man with the tweed cap was silent. Met by the impasse of Mary's nationality, he sat absorbed in his own thoughts. Finally he said, So you're not Canadian what are you? Mary had been looking in the mirror behind the bar and so did not catch this last question. He repeated it. She answered that she was an American, but her father was a Norwegian. He died several years ago. A Norwegen! Hah. Me, I'm Swedish. Norweganser no good! Oh? she said, My father was nice. Well, that's just because he was your father, he replied, his jaw set firm. That don't make Norwegians good. Are you married? he asked. Yes I am, to the man sitting next to me. And so that went, the Swede asked more questions and was generally skeptical of the couple's local residence. To him they remained Canadian. This word, along the coast from Blaine to Seattle, is commonly used to mean "odd ball."

The Swede said, Well, I'm a bachelor, wouldn't have it any other way. I work up in the woods, I save my money. I worked up there thirty years now and I saved plenty. Seeing her chance to annoy the man Mary said, Well, if that's the case, perhaps you'll buy the whole place a drink? Wall, hell no I won't! was the Swede's reply. He grew expansive at this point, about how people should live and how they should stick to business and not go around expecting to be bought drinks, and how if you did not watch your step you would meet shiftless people who did not save their money, everywhere.

But anyway, the Swede added at last, You're Canadian! I know damn well ya are! Yes, Mary answered softly, the very beginnings of tears in her eyes, We're Canadian, we're very Canadian. Well, Me! he said, slapping his chest, I'm American. Yes, I can see that, Mary said.

She went over to the booth were Carl was talking to Leonard and his wife. Leonard was saying, But shitchew can't fool around with that laborin' there's nothin' in that. Carl answered that for all the time he had spent at the hall he had not gotten any work yet so it was hardly a matter of having fooled around with it anyway. Leonard said, Yes I know, but shitchew have to get in with somebody, you know that. I ought to getchew on with me finishin' concrete. There's where the pay is. Shitchew won't work half the time at that laborin' anyway, you know that. Shideye make sixty dollars a day ora don't think I done anything. Then Leonard sucked a little air through his teeth, raising his upper lip ever so slightly, and showing his gold tooth. This was his habit after saying something.

His wife was like a kewpie doll, a pleasant girl, much younger than he. She said, Aw Leonard, buy another drink. He grinned. Shitchew don't want another drink do you? and laughed to Carl. She said,

Aw Leonard, Honey, get everybody a drink. She liked
to see him spend his money; their little house was
filled with the things he had bought her. There were
clocks with dogs standing over them, clocks with
house plants growing out of them, clocks that were
airplane propellers. Leonard thought a great deal of
his wife.

   After ordering another round, Leonard sucked
a little air through his teeth and continued, Shitchew
oughta see the money I got in my deep freeze, yaw
that's right, funny place to keep it ain't it? It's froze
solid. But hell, I can lock the deep freeze. There was
a slight pause, and then he said, Shideye never trusted
banks. Jimmy Frazer came through the door. He truly
was a Canadian, an Indian, who looked to be
half-breed, his chin weak and receding a little too
much. Carl went over to talk to him. He asked Jimmy
how his wife was. Oh, she's O.K. She's still taking it
pretty hard, Christ I been bothered by those funeral
home guys, you know they put the baby in a four
hundred dollar casket. A little baby like that. You
know I never even got a chance to ever see her alive.
I didn't know what to say, I wanted to see her buried
right, but I don't know. I told those guys I couldn't
pay 'em and they said I could take my time. I don't
know whether they'll try to get it from the county or
not, I guess not, they said I'd have to try to pay the

bill. It seems, Carl said, that it could have been done with less expense. How are the other kids? O.K. Bobby got that pneumonia too, but it looks like he's going to come out of it. He finished his beer quickly and said, Why don't you take a walk with me over to the house for a minute, I want to go check on Clara, and see if the stove's O.K.

Carl told Mary where he was going. Jimmy's house was two blocks away, by the tracks. The McCartys entered The Savoy as Carl and Jimmy left. As they walked, Carl asked Jimmy if he had had much to do lately. Oh, I did some junkin' for Masters, but hell we didn't get enough to make it worth while. I stripped some motors for him. Last week I worked a day for Wilson on a roof and made twenty dollars, but hell that one day at a time don't mean nothing. I was thinking of going back to Chilliwack. Clara's mother has a little shack there. I can't make the rent on this house. The old lady's been pretty good, but she was complaining because I'm so far behind in the rent. I can't do the work I was supposed to on it. They had reached the house. The fire was low and it was chilly inside. Jimmy brought in some wood from a pile of scrap. The flue did not draw well, something was wrong with it. There were three rooms. The parents used one for a bedroom. There was a kitchen, and the front room. Carl built a fire in the cookstove while Jimmy fixed the fire in the heating stove. Clara was in bed not feeling well, but when they arrived she got up and smiled. She wore a chenille housecoat. She had a soft quiet voice. Her face was delicate and lovely, and seemed more Indian than her husband's. The children lay sprawled on a sofa, some sleeping, the littlest ones crying, all who were awake fitfully watching T.V. A set so dim it was barely discernible. There was the powerful smell of wet diapers and dirty babies, kerosene, gelatinous dishwater. The air was penetrated by the single bare bulb that burned in the kitchen and threw its weak shaft of light into the front room. The light fell on the dim T.V. and seemed to stay there fighting for supremacy. The snow had gone wholly to rain, its chill penetrated the little house. With the starting of the fires the air did not grow warm, but the acrid smell increased, now mixed with the wood smoke. Crackling noise and light, and the powerful, heady smell. Outside the wet chill threw itself against the sides of the house with, apparently, all the time in the world.

Carl went back to The Savoy. Jimmy said he had better stay there a while longer, he would come later. Mary was sitting with the McCartys. Leonard and his wife had gone elsewhere. The place was getting crowded. Ramona suggested going to the WhileAway for a beer and then going home. She said,

Damnit if we're caught in here at twelve o'clock all those idiots will try to kiss us. They sat for a while longer finishing their beers and James talked about Smith, the farmer. Hell, he said, Smith doesn't give a damn about cost, if he wants something he gets it, hah hah that's the difference. He got baby blue stuff for his toilet, ha ha, that's pretty different. Bet you never saw much of that. A baby blue toilet stool, who ever heard of that? Oh! James! They're going to crap in it, Ramona said, frowning, having difficulty focusing. You know that, I don't see what's so great about a baby blue crapper, she said, turning to Mary, laughing and dragging on her cigarette and at last laughing outright so that her whole body shook. James got a little hot about that. His cap was twisted to one side so that the bill stuck down over his ear. That's what's wrong with you, Ramona! That's where you don't get it! He was now shouting. That's where you're just a damn fool, Ramona, do you think Smith gives a damn what you think, you don't think that do you, hell no! he doesn't have to. He never will. He wouldn't even pick you up out of the street if you was Jesus Christ, Ramona! You're just an Esquimau. That's the difference. Ha Ha.

Ramona squinted and looked at Mary, finally she smiled slightly, Sure, James, sure. If I was Jesus Christ I'd kick Smith's ass!

Later, in the WhileAway, they met a man who was down from Nome on a three month vacation. He was a loudmouth who kept walking all over the tavern talking to the various patrons. Ramona had known him slightly. He was saying in his booming voice, By God we pick king crabs outa Norton Sound that're bigger than that Esquimau girl sittin' over there. James said, What if you took Ramona to Phoenix I'll bet they never saw an Esquimau there, ha ha, they wouldn't know what to think would they? He took short quick drinks from his glass, and stared out the window at the rain. That'd be pretty different. Bet they never saw an Esquimau. The loudmouthed man returned to their table and squeezed in with them, next to Ramona. He put his hand on her leg. Kumeeana! he said. That means Thank You in Esquimau, don't it kid, and he poked Ramona in the ribs with his elbow. Sure, Ramona responded, Koomaehnna! That means thank you, it means other things too. The man looked at her, not wanting to disclose that his knowledge of the language consisted only of a few unimportant words. He said, Sure, sure. That's what it means. You know I feed reindeers for the government up there. Been working eighteen months steady, decided to come down here for my vacation. See a lotta Esquimaux. We take hay and grain out on the Barrens when the weather gets hard. Make a lotta money, I can't stand to see those guys down here strugglin' year in year out not making any headway. Boy, I wouldn't trade places withem for anything.

You prick, Ramona said softly. What? the man asked. Oh, I didn't say anything, Ramona answered, smiling at Mary. The man continued, Say, what happened to that man you was with when I saw you down in Seattle? Didn't he work at Boeings? Oh, he dropped dead one day, Ramona laughed. See he got run over by an airplane. The man took that with a slight false chuckle and looked down at his beer, saying, Well, you wouldn't recognize Nome no more, changed a lot since you was there. We have a lot of trouble with the Esquimaux. They're pretty shiftless. Can't keepem from killing the reindeers, they won't send their kids to school. Seems like they don't wanta learn. They still trade their wives, can't teachem nothin' about how to live. Say, you wouldn't care to go out to the car for a drink wouldja? Ramona looked at him trying to focus, What the hell, man, why don't you buy us a drink right here? Sure, he said, I'll buy *you* a drink. No, boooolshit, buy us all a drink, she said. Hell I don't wanta buy everybody a drink, he answered, and left. Over at the bar he was standing by two men who were seated. He was looking back at Ramona, smiling, the two men were laughing, nothing could be heard of what they said.

• 131

Shortly after that the little group left the WhileAway. They were going to stop by the Wymans for a final New Year's Eve beer and then the McCartys were going back out to the pea-shack. It continued a cold wet night. In the shadows of the streetlights the vast drooping and ascending boughs of the great western cedar, the black asymmetrical hemlock. The heavy misty rain lay on them like a mantle.

It was four o'clock in the morning when the McCartys left the Wymans' house. They went out the back door to their old car. Ramona lurched in the doorway, feeling with one foot for the steps. In the back of the car the babies were crying. Mary had wanted to take them into the house but Ramona said they're asleep, covered them with the blanket. James felt for the edge of the door, his face was gray and crumbling, a disintegrated cast. He began talking, Ramona! Stop that kid! Why don't you take care of him? Ramona was feeling for the door handle, swaying, she fell against the side of the car. She coughed, her one lung struggled in the night air. She could hardly get her breath. Coughing, holding her hand at her mouth, she swore softly. James, on his side was having trouble gripping the door handle, he had a hold on it but seemed unable to open it. For a very long time they stayed thus, Ramona coughing and James staring at the handle not being able to make his hand work it. A cock crowed somewhere in the distance through the eternal rain. A smell of dung came through the evergreen boughs from across the empty lot where the old lady kept cows. Again the cock crowed. Up on the hill back of the house the trees there swayed in the storm that was not a storm but a routine of the winter, as thoughtless as a saying, dreadful in the long run, and as irresistible as a music lying over the land. The thick clogged second growth around the feet of the greater trees caught the whole element and made of it a black mesh, forever dripping.

Ramona! he shouted, Goddamnit get in the car. She did not move. Her eyes were sealed. She breathed as though asleep, self-contained. Her lips moved when James shouted. The late traffic could be heard, and the lights seen, over on the logging truck cutoff two blocks away. Goddamnit, Ramona, you could get into bed, why don't you get in the car. What do you want, Ramona, a guy here, is that what you want. That's all you can do Ramona, get into bed. That's what you do. You're just a primitive. Why don't you pretend the car's a bed, Ramona, and get in it. Ha. Let's go, Ramona. Come on. He finally got his door open. He reached over and opened the door on

Ramona's side. Come on, he said, get in here. Oh James, why don't you shut up, you make me sick. You make me sick, James, she shouted. Who the hell are you, you think you're so great. You think you're pretty damn great don't you. Well you're just an asshole. You know that James, that's what you are. James had started the car. The motor ran roughly with a very uncertain idle and in the wet air the exhaust lay on the ground, a sharp, persistent smell. Another cock crowed. James said What do you want to do, Ramona? Get out of here, James, what's wrong with you? Do you know what's wrong with you, Ramona, he asked barely audible. Why don't you shut up, James, why don't you just shut up. What's wrong with you, James, give me that baby, put him down, what's wrong with you. James put the baby in the back seat. Davie was screaming. Ramona went through a spell of coughing but more quietly this time. That's the difference, James said, You know what you do, Ramona: You're just a cunt that's all. Booooolshit, she said softly, you assole, that's all you are, I know you, that's what you are, why don't you go take a crap in Smith's toilet. Haha James, that's what you oughta do. He put the car in gear and eased out on the clutch. The car crept ever so slightly forward. He wanted to back out of the driveway. He put the car in gear again and eased out on the clutch.

The car crept forward. He let out on the clutch again and the car went forward. Finally he got it in reverse and backed out slowly. They were shouting to one another as they drove off.

QUIET DAYS

During the early spring Carl met Leonard
AND LEARNED THAT THE KEWPIE DOLL HAD LEFT HIM.
She ran off with a younger man, the man was not
the wage earner Leonard was, certainly, and Leonard
had sent them some money once or twice. They had
gone to California. Leonard took a fatherly attitude
toward the affair, and hoped his wife would tire of
her fling and come back. Carl also had his hopes
renewed by Leonard that he would get some work.
Leonard had said, I'll see what I can do. You just sit
tight.

The McCartys had moved to their place in the
country. It was a farmhouse that at one point was
probably used for a son, or a hired man. It was off the

highway about a quarter of a mile on the way to Cedar Mills.

Some days that spring were bright. The overriding moisture left and the days were sometimes full of sun; sharp, cold, almost dry air lay over that small land and it was a hopeful time. Nonetheless, the McCartys' stay there seemed predicated on more than they were capable of. James had quit his job as flunky carpenter with the Farmer Smith. Whether he had quit or the farmer had simply run out of work for him was not at all clear. Anyway, he seemed quite happy and Ramona certainly was. A move in itself can be bright and hopeful, and so the days moved by.

The cherry trees bloomed. And there was a pear tree. And several apple trees. There was space for a garden and James cleared that, raking the dead overlay in piles and burning it. The smoke had a fine nostalgic smell, and James, shifting his cigar in his mouth, would stand by the piles with the rake, lifting bits from the edge into the fire. Carl broke a spring on his car and mentioned it to James. James invited him out to fix it in his garage, saying he had a lot of tools and would show him how, that it would be easy enough. They went to a junk yard and got a used spring. The McCartys were drinking much less. It was a nice time. Even some of the things in James' sense of humor that had irritated Carl, were different now. For instance, as Carl was removing the last nut, the spring broke loose and buried itself in the ground, a breath away from Carl's hand. James laughed. He said, Wow you almost got it that time ha ha, I guess you didn't have all the tension off the spring. You should of lifted the car more.

As for Ramona, she changed less in temperament than her husband. But she too grew quieter, and though never an untidy woman, and primitive peoples generally do fear dirt, especially Esquimaux, she kept a very neat house now that she had one, strictly speaking.

There is a nice humanity inferred by a house. The sun streams in the window. Out through the windows one can see something of the surroundings. James was working on the yard, pruning the trees. Ramona got better. She did not cough so violently or so often. She sewed some, for the children and herself. She knitted James a nice wool cap, the children some wool house slippers. She showed them to Mary the first day the Wymans called, and they both marveled at them. An Indian woman in the camp had showed her how to do it. Her smile was even more beautiful those days. Soon the trees began to bloom and then to leaf. All things again began to grow possible. Once in a while when the Wymans went to call, and they did often, they would pick The

Old Man up along the road and take him along with them. Sometimes he would be going to Cedar Mills but it never made much difference. He would sit in a rocking chair by the window and smile and nod as he rocked. He said nothing although he did address Ramona upon arrival and again at departure. The children would jump out of the car and head for the trees which they loved to climb, the littlest one standing around the base of the tree looking up into the branches, talking to the others, who were climbing.

James expected to go to work on one of the new dam sites up the river. The season for that work was starting and a number of carpenters would be called. There was some concern with how he should get the money to get his tools out of hock, but even that seemed possible and could be let go until the time came. He had worked the spring before and they were expecting any day to receive the money back from the income tax form he had filed. Because he had not, of course, made enough money to have to pay taxes, they would get about seventy dollars back, they thought. Every day Ramona went to the mailbox on the highway to look for it.

In that early springtime some of the days were

not so cold, midday was beginning to be warm. Then they would take trips around the countryside with the Wymans. Carl was spending his days at the union hall waiting around for the chance to join. From his work at the chicken farm he had carefully saved the seventy-five dollars "initiation fee" against such a chance . . . but there were days when he would decide not to spend his time there, and then they would sometimes go out to the McCartys' place, and from there the two families would go over to Log Lake to let the children wade in the water. They would have a six-pack of beer and lie on the beach, talking. There was a concession stand and they bought the children some ice cream or candy. Log Lake was an old logging town surrounded by hills of slash and second growth. James, with grins and disparaging remarks about himself, and about the foolishness of such activity, would take off his shirt to get a little sun. He may have been embarrassed about the peculiarity of his chest. Nevertheless he made the most of the sun, cigar in mouth, and cap on head. They laughed a lot. The tribulations of the children were better handled at those times too. When one of them came crying back to the little group of adults on the blanket, with a hurt finger, or a cut, the child would be well received. The parents were at peace. This is not to say that the children were all that ignored or maligned at other times, but that the whole form had an accord. Those were happy days.

One Friday afternoon they decided to dig clams and this time they went directly to the beach. Most of the beaches in those parts have been clammed out. Butter clams are scarce. There are a few razor clams. They did get a few butter clams and roasted them in a fire on the beach. Most people do not much like horse clams, which are gross and tough, a long thick neck extending out of the shell. Some of them weigh four or five pounds. They make a very passable chowder though, and the two families brought a quantity of those back with them. They cleaned them in the Wymans' back yard. During the cleaning Ramona ate small bits smiling as she did so and offering pieces to the children.

The McCartys waited and waited for their tax refund but it never came. Ramona went faithfully to the mailbox every day, but the check never came. The Wymans arrived one day just as she had started down the road to the mailbox. James was reading a magazine. He got up when they arrived and fixed the stove, which was an oil drum with a flue hole cut in the side near the end. It sat horizontal, on welded legs. There was a door cut in the front. He threw a few sticks of wood in it, trimmings he had saved when he pruned the fruit trees. How are you all? he said with a smile.

Have a seat. The children ran outside. Look here, he said to Carl, I've just been reading an article about Henry Ford. Boy, he was a mean son of a bitch wasn't he? Carl looked at the magazine, it showed pictures of Henry Ford at various times in his life, as a young man, as a young inventor, married, as a young successful businessman, as a mature man, with his wife both a little older, and finally as a thin scrawny old man standing in front of one of his cars. That's some article, James said. Carl was still looking at it.

The Wymans had brought a gallon of wine, which the McCartys did not like to drink but would if there were nothing else. James got some glasses. Ramona returned from the mailbox with a letter, it was not the check but nevertheless she was pleased because it was from her sister who was living in Nome and she had not heard from her in a long time. She sat in the middle room, at the table, reading. Every now and then she laughed. Gosh. Do you know what she says? She might get to go to Seattle this summer, some of the girls from her school are gonna be taken to Seattle on a trip this summer. Gosh, wouldn't . . . and then Ramona stopped and looked out the window. She sat for several minutes very still, looking out the window. At last she put the letter down and said, Wouldn't that be wonderful.

• 143

By The River

Carl Wyman had begun to get a job now AND THEN AT THE UNION HALL. THE JOBS WERE FOR NO more than one day. Some lasted only a half day. An afternoon. Now he sat around at the union hall rather than the unemployment office. It was an altogether different group of people at the union hall. Far from the downtrodden, gaunt men at the state office, these men at the union disparaged all that degraded seeking after anything that came along. They spoke in such terms as "wage" and "conditions" but for all that, most of them got no more work than their less fortunate brothers over at the office. Of course the union members would not for anything have considered those tramps as brothers. The common laborer then made two dollars and ninety cents an hour in the union. The going rate out of the state office was one dollar an hour, sometimes a dollar and a quarter an hour. It may seem incredible, but there are a class of men who find it impossible to put their hands on a seventy-five dollar initiation fee. If anyone needs reminding, possible means "able to be." The two groups of workers in this case did not really differ, except for that.

Wyman found it no more possible at the union hall to ingratiate himself with the man at the window than he had at the state employment office with the man at the counter. He spent much of the time inside, in the meeting room, sitting on the seats. There were a few calls for men most every day, but in any case he had not been a member long enough to be considered. He heard from some of the other new members that they had been let in simply as a device to put more money into the treasury, and that indeed there was not, and never would be, enough work in that area to allow the younger members to earn a living wage, as it was called. But rumors were so manifest in the union hall that Carl neither honored nor discounted that last bit of information.

The men at the union hall tended to look well.

That is, not sick, as so many of the men did in the unemployment office. Their complexions were better. This could not have been because they found themselves more in the out-of-doors. It looked like these members were, on the average, better fed. There were some fat ones among them. The fat man at the unemployment office would have been stared at. On their backs were untattered clothes. Is there even a nomenclature for such stuff? There were jackets of bright red and black checked wool plaids, long like car coats, there were shorter ones of gabardine, well lined, with zippers.

One spring day Carl stood outside the union hall on the sidewalk, ready to go home. The sun was bright. He had been inside for three hours that morning and it looked as if there would be no more calls. A fat, dirty Hudson pulled up on the other side of the street. Billy Hendersson got out and stuck a key into the door, locking it. He walked across the street toward Carl. They spoke. Billy went on into the union hall. Carl saw him talking to the man at the window. When Billy came out, he stood by Carl. Several other men were standing on the sidewalk. Any luck? Carl asked him. No. Hell I thought that refinery over at Anacortes was gonna start up but they keep saying next week, sometime next week. Well, Carl said, I heard they had a little work over there but they haven't made any big calls. By the way, he added, I saw you last fall I think it was, at the unemployment agency with a little old man, you were pretty mad. Oh! Ya, Billy said, Was you there that day? Jesus did you hear the way that bastard talked. Wasn't that rich? You know that poor old guy had a hard time of it last winter. He didn't get any work at all. He's my neighbor, he lives down the road from me in the brush. He's got twelve kids, and they're all nice kids, a couple of his older boys come over and help me get in firewood. I got a chainsaw, so we fallem and buckem up and I give them a share of it.

As Hendersson spoke a man in a blue suit and shiny necktie came around the corner off the side street. When he saw Billy he stopped short and went over to him. He said, Say, aren't you Hendersson? Billy was chewing on a toothpick. He took a long look at Carl and then looked back at the man. Nooo, he said, I'm not Hendersson. The man looked at him sharply, his eyebrows lifted and went together. He said, Oh, sure, you're Hendersson. And you

know me, don't you. You remember me. Billy replied,
No, I sure don't, I never saw you in my life. Now
come on, the man said, I sold you a washing ma-
chine. Oh, that's juicy, I never bought a washing
machine. You don't know what you're talking about.
And I never saw you in my life. The man had backed
away a half step. He looked at Billy. At length he
said, You know, you're not fooling anybody. You
know damn well you recognize me. Billy began to
get a little red in the face. Huh UH! he said, I never
saw you before. You got the wrong guy. I hope
you don't hound everybody like that. At that the
man smiled maliciously. Well you know, he said,
you're not going to get by with this, I'll have the credit
bureau take your pay if you ever work. With this last
statement   the   man   looked   around   at   the
rest of the men on the sidewalk. They were not much
interested, only a couple of them had bothered to pay
any attention to the conversation. Yow, and I'll sue
you for mi-misrepresentation, you fool, I don't e-even
know your name! Billy replied, his face by now deep
red, the sweat stood on his forehead below the leather
band of his hard hat. The man said no more and
moved on down the street.

    Who was that! Carl said. Have you ever seen
that man? Hendersson stared down the street after

the man. He watched him as he turned the next corner. Yow. I know him, he said. Sure. I know that bastard, I know him very well. The toothpick had stopped working in his mouth. He just stared down the street, toward Main Street. Carl drew back slightly. He stared at Hendersson. A few minutes went by. Billy suggested they walk toward the river.

As they sat down on the concrete wall above the river Carl asked Billy if he expected any trouble from the washing machine man. Naw, Hendersson said, he's been after me for two years. I bought a washing machine from him and couldn't make the final payment. We're using it. What am I supposed to do, give it back? Give it back and have that sonofabitch sell it as a used machine when I'm still paying for it. That makes sense doesn't it! He gets three and a half times what it cost instead of two and a half. I wouldn't give that man or his employers the skin off my ass!

Carl was staring into the river. That makes sense, he said at last. Across the river was a thicket of trees. Below, along the bank, a collection of small boats. They bobbed against the down river current. The sky had become a pearl grey. Whether or not it would rain was a real but unimportant question. Carl said, Well, what the hell, he has lots of people like you to bother. Hendersson looked at him and smiled. Exactly, he said. Have you had much work out of the hall? Carl asked. Oh, no not much. Hendersson said, looking away, down the river and chewing on his toothpick, But enough to keep going. I don't need much. I mean, I need more, but I get enough work. Been on any long jobs? I was on a job once for three weeks, Hendersson answered. There was quite a bit of overtime so I made about a hundred and forty a week. One week, actually it was the last check which was for a little more than a week, I made one-seventy-five. Where do you live, Carl asked. Oh, it's just a shack really, it's unfinished on the inside and it's got the tarpaper on the outside. I'm supposed to finish it off and then the old lady that owns it will want rent I suppose. I keep puttin' her off, for obvious reasons, he said, and laughed. But you oughta come out there sometime. When I made all that money I bought a cute little horse. His name's Buckshot. And I bought a saddle. I got him from a man over by Cedar Mills. Well sure, I'd like to go out there, where is it? Well, you know where Barn's Angus Ranch is? You turn up the hill there as if you were gonna go to Macton and it's the third road back into the brush on your right, it looks like an old logging road and we live back on that road about, oh, I'd say a little more than a quarter of a mile. You'll see the house easy because you come out into a clearing after a while. O.K., Carl said, are you going to be over here tomorrow? Yes, I'll come over in the morning. Well, if we don't get sent out in the morning, why don't we drive out to your place together, I'd like to see your horse. That's great, Billy replied.

They sat looking at the river. When did you join the union, Billy asked. About a month ago. When did you join? Last fall. Carl asked, Is it true what I heard, that in order to get a good, long job you have to pass around a few bottles, to the right people? Oh, I don't know. I've heard that too. I could believe anything about those pricks in there. But I never did it. I haven't had too many jobs but they send me out quite a bit. It might be true . . . who's to say? But you know, they're all petty thieves. That's petty thievery. I don't mean just the union officials. The businessmen, the clerks, those guys at the unemployment office. They're all petty thieves, they hit the poor working man for anything they can get, peanuts! So what if they take a bottle now and then? That just means they ain't got the guts to demand five bucks from you at the window. And if they did have guts, that's what they'd do—they'd say here's a job you can have this morning, that'll be five bucks. One thing they do that's pretty juicy though, you ever heard about that? Well, every Thanksgiving and Christmas they have a turkey raffle, you know, you buy a ticket with a number on it. And then there's a drawing. Every damn time all the officials big and little get a turkey. What do you think of that! Now there's some gall I can respect. Whew! But hell. What's the difference— over at the unemployment office they may not take bribes, at least I never heard of it. No, over there they expect you to suckass, that's worse. What part of the country do you come from, Billy asked. Illinois. Oh? Is that so? I come from Wisconsin. What part? Outside of Madison, I was raised on a farm mostly but there were times my dad lived in town. Did you come here from Wisconsin? Yeah, I been here twice. A couple of years ago I came out here but I couldn't get a job. I got a cousin in Cedar Mills, we stayed with them. Jesus, that last winter we spent in Wisconsin was bitter cold. That was a year ago this winter.

They watched the traffic. It was a day when many men came to see what was happening, if anything, at the union. The gulls dipped over the river, sometimes they dropped suddenly upon it. Awkward, searching birds. Sometimes they would rise a foot above the water and dive suddenly under, only their wing tips showing. Carl tried to determine whether or not they came up with live food or refuse. Some of them were glaucous gulls. Mostly they were herring gulls. There was a dump across the river. A boring fascination. The constant parasitism held his attention. The quarreling, the endless short flights. Very busy creatures. At the far bend of the river, south, a tug and barge came on. The gulls strung themselves out above it like dull sheets of white paper. Their screams were lost in the distance.

But god that was a cold winter, Billy went on. I tore half the side out of the barn to get wood to keep us warm. I'd go out to start the car and the oil would be so stiff the starter wouldn't even turn it over. There was a poor horse out in the barn lot was so stiff and cold he wouldn't move all day, he'd have ice hanging all over him, from his ribs and tail, and his chin, he looked like a cold old man with a beard. Big balls of ice hanging all over him and balls of ice under his feet. I wonder if that makes their hooves cold, all that ice packed in under there? I don't know, Carl said. You like horses a lot? Oh sure, I guess I do, when I was a kid I ran away on one, that was when we lived on a farm. I was on my way to Alaska. I thought, I always wanted to go to Alaska. Well how did you go, Carl interrupted, along the roads? How did you ever expect to make it? Oh, I just went across fields, right straight, or what I thought was straight. But I didn't make it. I got to some place in Minnesota, I think it was close to Redwing. The weather was terrible. Just terrible. But not as bad as it was when we started back here last winter. Before we left we were all in bed all day to keep from freezing. I got out of bed once a week to go to town to get the relief check and bring back something to eat.

They parted, agreeing to meet the next day. Billy got into his car and drove off, waving. He was hunched over behind the wheel, favoring his bad shoulder by relaxing against the door. Carl walked back past the union hall. A heavy-set man ran around the corner almost bumping into him. The man stepped back quickly like a boxer and pulled his baseball cap off and shouted, Hi bub! Where you goin'. Carl stared at the man. The man stuffed his baseball cap into his back pocket. He continued to dance around. He said, Hey bub, you got a smoke? Carl said Sure, here. The man took the cigarette from the package. He spilled several on the sidewalk and apologized elaborately. Where's the goddamn action? he asked. Action? It looks like you've got all the action in this town, Carl answered. Ha. That's pretty good, say bub what's your name anyway? Carl. Carl? Huh. That's pretty good. My name's John. Yeah that's me, John. I'm a Chicago Buster. You get that? I just blew inta this fuckin' burg. And you say there's no action, eh? Well that's too bad. You got any food on ya? Like a sandwich? I got the squirms. I been dynamitin' every town up the coast. Say where do you live? You know your way around in this town? John asked, ignoring Carl's answer, and continuing, You say there's no action eh, what dya mean? Well, just that, Carl said, that there's no action. No action uh? No action. No action. Come on, where's the goddamn action! Listen! Carl said, There is *no* action. None whatever. Except maybe right here where we're standing. You want another cigarette, sure here. But that's it. And I don't know exactly what you mean by that but I assure you there is no action. Hey, wait a minute, John said, there's a live butt, I'll save it for later. Well, bub what do ya say we get a beer. O.K., that sounds good, Carl replied. I'm gonna blow this burg fast, John said as they walked off.

THE DEER

Carl did not meet Billy the next day. They
DID NOT MEET AGAIN FOR SEVERAL WEEKS. BOTH OF
them were put to work for a series of very short jobs.
Things began to pick up. By the time Carl went out to
see the Henderssons, Billy had called at the Wymans'
house several times. That year, in the state of Washing-
ton, there was before the legislature one of those bills,
number 202, that are said to be "right to work" bills.
In any case, the question is loaded and disposes itself
along seemingly straight lines: does a man have the
right to work for anyone he pleases, and does he have
the right to do so independently. The question is never,
of course, Is this a wise thing to do? The "right" part
of it gets emphasized. But enough of that. The point

is that Hendersson, being a good union man, got himself scores of stickers from the union and placed them all over his car, even against the undercarriage. Vote Against 202 they read. The Wyman children when seeing his car come down the road would shout Here comes 202! The sign read VOTE AGAINST 202, in luminescent lettering. Yellow against black.

Billy suggested to Carl that they might poach a deer. He had already gotten one near the house one evening. So Carl took a trip out to the Henderssons. When Carl got there Billy was cutting some firewood with his chainsaw. It was late afternoon. The sun was low in the sky and the day was normal—overcast, a grey, high light. The sun would set in a half hour, a thin clarity on the horizon. For the brief time there were the great lengths of its red arms extending over the tops of the rife second growth, past the balanced crown of the cedar and the ragged point of the hemlock. A dark, black-green and a burnt-out red. The tangled grass of the clearing bent this way and that, spread out in the half light. Billy stopped working and looked up when Carl drove in. It was his habit to greet one always as if it were the first meeting, very pleasant. He said, Oh hello! How are you! It's good you came out today. I was expecting you. Let's go over and see the horse before it gets dark. And then he wiped his forehead with his handkerchief. Hi Billy, you think we'll get a deer tonight? I don't know, Billy answered, It looks like it might clear. When Carl got out of his car they started walking toward the barn.

The barn was tall. Everything on this place was ramshackled. The barn wore the rays of the sun through its loose boards, and its cedar shake roof was full of holes. Buckshot turned out to be a very extraordinary horse. As Carl looked at him, he wondered why a sensible man would buy such a thing. The creature was boney, undersized, roman nosed, of very questionable temper—neither a horse nor a pony, neither normal nor quite to be ignored, but rather that four-legged thing with a "character," utterly unuseable. Buckshot certainly needed care, his hooves were so long they had split almost up to the quick.

Now the sun was gone. Billy's wife had come out to the railing where they stood. Carl had never met her. The light at that moment was silver as it grew darker, and the skeletal barn grew more substantial when the structure of it asserted its proportions in the waning light of the sun. Inside there were some scattered bales of old hay, mildewed and useless now. The forest of low heavy second growth lay as a barrier, its single trees undifferentiated in the diminished day.

They got back to the house and went in. Billy asked Carl if he had had anything to eat, and Carl said that he had had supper before coming out. Billy said he had eaten earlier too. . . . The children were running through the house playing cowboy and Indian. Two boys. One was about four and the other was six. Next year the six year old would start to school. As one entered the house the sink with a bucket under it was on the left near the door. Straight beyond the other two rooms opened out, there was an unfinished wall between them. The smell was enough to discourage a strong man. The wife said Look! I've got some biscuits. Carl again insisted he'd had enough to eat at supper. Billy took him into the other part of the house where for some time they looked at Billy's guns. He had several pistols and two rifles. Carl glanced around the room. In one corner there was a double bed, it was away from the walls a little too far to seem natural. The two boys slept on two cots that were placed out of line at the other end of the room. The smell was always present. Carl noticed a shelf of books and when Billy had gone back into the kitchen to speak to his wife, he looked at them. They were an utter miscellany. Pulp mysteries and detectives, *Huckleberry Finn,* and Engels' *Anti-Duhring.* There were also several volumes of Stoddard's travels.

They went out the door, both carrying rifles,

under the partly clear, breaking sky. They walked toward the barn, its latticed members shone almost black and white in the shadows from the moon. The moon rode above its roof, full. Billy was talking about Wisconsin. Growing in a broad swath out of the impenetrable second growth a cloud stretched toward the zenith. Carl looked for the Dipper and Orion. As they walked along Billy wondered aloud if they would get a deer. He thought it probable. He held forth on the subject of when a deer is best to get anyway, saying that the regular season was the worst time to kill one. The Fall was the time they were in the worst condition. And so they went past the barn and past the blackberry brambles that edged the clearing and finally they were on a trail into the deep underbrush.

Very quickly they came to another much smaller clearing. There was a small body of water standing in it. It was surrounded by marshy ground. Billy, Carl said, you can't really live this way now, you know. Silence. They skirted a grove of black birch. Why not? Well, it wouldn't ever be possible to make it for long. I've known a thousand guys like you. They thought they could get by in a minimal, I mean, by the least way possible, and they all ended getting a steady job somewhere, and it was because in the end they saw that it was more work to fight it than give in to it. The world is *not* what it was once Billy, you read about all those ways men lived in the past and it sounds good, and it must have been good, but we don't know even what that means. God-damnit, like us now, for instance, we're walking single file through growth that is far too thick for us to see even a foot, and we're walking single file. O.K. So what does that mean. In fifteen minutes we could be out of it. I mean if we walked back to your place, in fifteen minutes we'd be in town. In a bar. You know that? As we walk along there are people sitting on their asses not giving a damn about a deer to feed themselves, not caring that the moon is shining, not caring about anything, they're just sitting there talking the same old shit that's been talked since who the hell cared.

There was a long silence. They walked the trail single file. Oh to hell with all that, Billy said at last, I don't see what that has to do with us, let 'em, I mean the world hasn't pressed into this second growth yet, and if I can't hear it I can't see it. Another long silence. They had come to a place where the trail was not so clear. The moon, too, was of little help by this time, they were so deep into the forest of brush. Carl said, Anyway, Billy, I've heard that if you *hear* a deer in this shit you'll never be able to *see* it, I mean not over ten feet away. Don't shoot me, please. Oh, you probably don't make the same sound a deer does, Billy answered.

There were spots in the forest that were so thick they were black, and then there were those spots that were thin, in which there was a weak kind of shadow. They stumbled over things that seemed rotten logs four feet thick, left there years ago by loggers. Cedar tends to shatter when felled. Do you know where we are going, asked Carl. Ya, I think we just keep walking and finally after about an hour in this direction we'll come out into a field. We can go there, and them come back, and if we don't see a deer in that time it's enough of a night. Their flashlight had failed. Their hands were numb with a kind of penetrating wet cold, and they stumbled on. They had on long, wool underwear so did not really feel the damp pneumonia air around them. A wind had begun to blow up.

But I haven't heard any sounds, Carl said. There hasn't been any sounds in this woods, Billy! just us walking along. We're not going to get a deer. Who the hell wants a deer anyway. Jesus, Billy, I mean the idea of killing a deer illegally appeals to me, but all those pricks with their vacations have already killed 'em. I mean they came out in their blazers and methodically killed 'em. Oh bullshit, it isn't much farther, Billy said. Just then a large branch fell off one of the tallest trees and came clipping down through the leaves. Watch it! Billy shouted. Carl jumped to the side. Wow. Jesus Christ! I've heard about widder makers but I never saw one, Carl said catching up with Billy. Well, if you see 'em it's O.K., said Billy.

I think a deer could be goosing me and I wouldn't know the difference, Carl continued. Billy found himself getting very tense. He needed to get the deer more than Carl did. In a sense Carl was just there for kicks, but finally Carl would survive without the fresh meat. Billy had noticed at those times when he called on the Wymans that they usually had fresh fruit. For instance they had oranges. The Henderssons at most times lived in great poverty, the one worry Billy had for his kids was whether or not they got enough oranges. He had heard vaguely, through the state agencies or in some other manner, that children ought to have fresh fruit in the long dark northwest winter. He thought of vitamin C. Carl was talking on the absurdity of looking for a deer in those limitless thickets. Billy thought of his kids' gums. They were ripe. Their smiles were ready enough but their gums were ripe. Red, very red. As he stumbled over a dead white larch log he stopped, and turned to Carl saying, What the hell are you bitching about? If you want to go back, go back. Go back! Carl shouted, Where the hell is back. I don't know, and I'd

bet you don't either. We haven't even made it to that
so-called clearing yet! On they walked, stumbling. At
times they warned each other to keep the gunbarrels
out of the mounds of earth pushed up by a rotted log.

After somewhat more than two hours they reached
the edge of the clearing. There were clouds in the sky.
They were fluffy and brilliant in the moonlight. When
the moon rode behind one of them the air grew heavy
with shade. The clearing was much larger than Carl
had expected. There were some buildings far across
the way. Carl asked what they were. Billy thought
they were the remains of an old farm. The land in the
clearing had the appearance of having been tilled. As
they walked toward the buildings they passed through
an orchard. Unpruned, the trees had grown to gro-
tesque proportions. The two men walked through
those sharp configurations in the moonlight, bending
down under the low branches.

Billy, you said you finally got to Alaska, when
was that? Let's see, he said, That must have been
about four or five years ago. How old were you?
Well, I'm twenty-five now, I was nineteen or twenty.
A sailboat was what screwed me up, imagine that, a
sailboat, kind of hard to imagine from where we're
standing now, eh. He laughed his short, high,

feminine laugh. His eyes were glistening. His face became reddish, the lips of his plum, babyish mouth curled and remained slightly apart. His tin hat shone in the brief moonlight. The moon was waning now, and the clouds were coming on a little thicker around the southwest horizon.

It was early summertime, I had a chance to ride over the Alcan with a guy from Madison, Billy continued, as they poked their heads in the first building they came to. They went about to the other buildings, examining the old, mildewed, useless gear that remained there. Ah, yes, my dream of going to Alaska finally came true. My old man kicked me out. Him? Oh, he was all right, but mostly a worthless bastard. Well, look, he was the kind of man that's pretty good in a way, he was always good to me, kind, he joked a lot, and he was a lot of kicks to be with when I was a kid. But he killed my poor damn mother. I never have forgiven him for that, although I don't know why I shouldn't, he's dead. Dead is forgiven anyway. He gave me a motorcycle when I was sixteen, but you know, the bastard stole it. I could never put that down, until they came after it. A brand new Harley. It was a beauty too. Blue and white. He drank, but he wasn't too much a drunk, he just made up for it with lying. I mean, he'd come home to my mom and tell her he'd been held up when the sonofabitch had spent most of his pay on some woman. Or I don't know what the hell he did with it, I don't think he gambled, he couldn't sit still long enough. One week he left for good, and when I used to see him in town he wouldn't speak to me. Once I started cussing him out, and you know, he pretended he didn't even recognize me. You know how fat I am now, well, I was that way when I was sixteen too, so I could wear his shirts. He left a lot of shirts. My mother went to work in a shirt factory in Madison, how about that?

But I got another motorcycle all right. I met an old woman who liked to be screwed, and she bought me lots of things. That was one of them. It was a Harley again, I ran it right into the ground, up and down the country roads, I didn't have nothin but the wind in my face. All day long. What do you mean, how old was she? Oh, she was old, if that's what you mean, she was about sixty-five. But how did that work? Well, so what, there was very little difference. She was just old that's all. She was enthusiastic and liked her screwing. I guess it was sort of like she was a mother, you know how that goes. But when I wasn't doing my job we talked a lot. She had a nice house, her husband was dead and she had a little money.

In fact, Billy said as they left the buildings and started across the clearing toward the edge of the forest, In fact I thought a lot of that old woman. There was one summer we went out to a lake north of Madison. She had a cabin. I couldn't see anything but riding my motorcycle, her sailboat didn't interest me at all. She liked to ride along on the sailboat. There was a couple of guys much older than me there, and she flirted with them a lot, and they were sort of suspicious of me. But I wasn't jealous. Actually I was a little bit. She had a way. I learned to run that boat, that's certain. Those guys kept ribbing me about the motorcycle, calling me a landlubber, so I learned to sail the boat. It was great. An altogether different kind of speed. We'd come around and she's scream like a little girl. We tacked up and down that lake all summer. It was a long narrow lake . . . it was very tricky. She had long black hair. Not many grey hairs. With combs she kept it in a knot at the back of her head. One gold tooth in front. Nice smile . . . she was hard to look at.

It had grown darker with the setting of the moon, but the clouds stayed along the horizon and the stars made enough light to give a remote visibility to things. She wrote me several letters when I was in prison, she was very disappointed with me for leaving in the first place, but the letters mostly chided me for getting into trouble. The edge of the forest was still some way ahead. They reminded each other that they had to keep an eye out for the barbed wire fence. Apparently there were some cattle in there but they had not seen any on their way to the clearing. You know, Billy said, I heard somebody had some steers in there but I haven't never seen one.

Billy resumed the conversation. I went to Alaska with that guy on the spur of the moment. It was the middle of winter, cold as hell, I got some money from the old woman to fix my motorcycle. I went across a ditch. I was going pretty fast but I fell off and just rolled down the bank, but the machine kept going and it was pretty clobbered up. I told her it was going to cost a lot more to fix it than it was, I always did that. I met that guy in a bar and we took off the next day. Carl interrupted. That was pretty sudden to decide such a thing wasn't it. Yow. It was. Sure, ya, look at my life now. I don't know. When you're young you go off, that's probably all there was to it. I told myself at the time I was tired of it all. It was very much like being kept in a cage. Or like one of those dummies that sit on laps, they talk, move, do anything, when you want 'em. But that wasn't it either. She used to try to get me to read certain books. Now I understand they were pretty good, but I couldn't see it then. They were, well, you know, they were all the English Works, I remember one, it was called *The Return of the Native*. Before I read it I

thought it was about Africa, you know, the return of
the native. But it wasn't. It was about England. It was
good too. But that wasn't what made me leave. I just
wanted to get away. Ya, you read that book.
Sometimes I remembert that guy working. Cutting
wood. But those women were funny weren't they?

Did you really want our cats for your dogs?
Carl asked as they were going across the fence. Sure!
Billy said. What the hell for? Oh, I don't know, I like
to chase cats I guess, and the dogs sure as hell do. But
you call them cat dogs, Carl said, what does that
mean, are there really cat dogs, I mean dogs that
chase cats professionally? Oh, I don't know about
professionally, but I think there are special dogs to
chase cats, and they're called cat dogs, and they do it
at night. At least that's what the man said. Carl,
you're sort of touchy about animals aren't you? I
mean you have some sort of idea that animals are
sacred, don't you. You think they should not be
killed, I got that idea, but you eat the meat, I've seen
you . . . what about that? They stood by the fence.
Carl had lit a cigarette. He smoked and looked at the
sky. Well I'm not clear there, Carl said, I never really
pretended to be, and anyway that's another question.
It just struck me as a weird idea that a man would
want to let cats loose for the express purpose of
putting dogs to them. After all, that is a little

tortured, if you want to compare it to my eating meat that's been killed by someone else. You might as well throw the cats directly to the dogs and be done with it. Why the chase? I guess it's the time interval that bothers me. It just seemed to me that the glee you'd derive from going through the woods after the cats *and* the dogs is something else, those are kicks you ought to get another way. After all, Carl concluded, There will be men to kill meat as long as there are men to eat it and vice versa. I don't lay any blame at the butcher's feet. He's simply a truck-driver in disguise. Billy laughed. What's that got to do with cats and dogs? I don't eat the cats, nor do I eat the dogs. At least I haven't yet. And anyway that's silly, what's the difference between chasing dogs that are chasing cats, and might not even catchem, I mean this time interval of yours, what's the difference, if a man kills a sheep, or a hog, and you eat it three weeks later, what's the difference, the thing's been killed! Billy was laughing.

They were deep in the forest now. Carl stopped. It had begun a light drizzle. The sky was completely obscured, but was not black yet, a high grey nothing. They were in a small clearing. Their faces were covered with a light film of water from the heavy mist. Of course, you're right, Carl said. Finally it is a question of whether or not one eats animals.

And it is true that it can't matter when they are killed. The act remains the same. The biologist may have a different term for those carnivores that eat dead as against those that eat live meat. But that's not a moral problem, that's a matter of classification. I don't think man in any sense comes under that, since he's making the classification. For instance, in the animal kingdom the problems are singular. Any being other than man has the problem of satisfying the demands of the next desire, there being two desires, presumably, consumption and reproduction. The standards for those demands may or may not come under the term survival of the fittest. After all, all that reasoning comes by way of man's hope to see it that way. I'm not at all convinced those animals, or even those men, who have survived, are the fittest. Are you? There was a silence. Carl continued, What disturbs me about the cats is that I have formed an attachment to them, though there was a desire on our part to get rid of them. We have too many. So I offer you some of them and you come up with the novel idea that you'd be very willing to take them because you have some cat dogs and you could use them. I meant the cat dogs could use them, Billy said with a smile. O.K., O.K., Carl went on, O.K., but you're not respecting my feelings about animals. You are talking about eating them, I'm talking about the sense of killing them, as an act of pleasure.

Look, I feel an urge when I'm trailing those dogs, I hear their bark, I fall over rotten logs, I get my face cut, I get worn out, I keep hearing the high bark of the dogs, I love that chase. What did you think you were going to do with those cats, Carl, drop them somewhere on a country road, what would chase them then? Some other dogs, or would they starve in some lonely barn begging milk from some goddamn farmer who'd recognize them and kick their asses out of his barn, huh! Billy was shouting now. They stopped on the trail, facing each other. Billy was holding his gun very tight, pointed at Carl. They stared at each other. In that moment Carl thought he would be shot. He thought that in another instant the trigger would be pulled and that would be the utter end of him. Good lord, he thought, this is absurd, why would I be shot in the middle of a deep woods? I have done nothing but live a very normal life. Normal life, he said to himself again in that brief instant. A very normal life. What the hell were you going to do with those cats, Carl. Oh, Jesus Christ, Billy! stop that. I thought you were going to let that thing go off. Carl climbed wearily over a fallen log. I think their chances will be better along the open road, he said. At least they might find a place to stay. You are just trying to justify your killing with the possibility that they might be killed anyway. But they might not be. They both sat down on the log. Billy said, But you think you can get rid of them, and you think somebody will take care of them.

No! I am saying that if you do give that generation back to the road it is no longer in your hands whether they survive or not. That with animals you don't intend to eat, that is, non-edible animals, a man is not responsible! I think this is the only proper use of the liberation you propose with your setting dogs to cats. But in that case it is very much planned and the cat probably hasn't got a chance. This is splitting hairs, Billy replied. So my use is not your use. He turned on the log and tried to get a look at the sky, he thought he could see a clear patch, and stars. Carl, unable to stop, went on, O.K., it is a fine point. In many ways perhaps it is men like us who have to be interested in fine points. So where does that get us, Billy said.

They sat on the log and finally Carl asked Billy if he knew the way back. Billy said he thought not. He did not recognize anything. He didn't know where he was. Carl thought he heard a sound. Like the breaking of a branch on the ground. Billy did too. They sat very still. They heard it again. They were tense, listening. Carl could find the north star by pointing from the Dipper, if he could only find the Dipper, he thought, at least they could walk in one direction. There was no possible way to get a bearing on where they were. They both heard the noise again. It made them a little uneasy but they remained on the log. Carl felt the log's bark with his fingers to determine what kind it was. From the feel of it, it was so smooth, he thought it was an alder. A rather big one.

Billy was fooling with his flashlight. It flickered once. I think it's the switch, Billy said. He continued to jiggle it, and started hitting it on the log. It came on, a bright shaft of light. Billy immediately switched it off. He switched it on again. It worked. Where do you think the sound came from, Billy whispered. Carl wasn't sure but he thought he sensed it directly back of them. They stood up carefully.

Both men stood peering into the darkness. Billy switched on the light and moved it very slowly in a semicircle to the right in back of where they stood and it came to rest with a little jerk on a pink white-faced steer. About two years old, Billy said. Ya, Carl answered. They both started moving forward, the light like a rope they were reeling in. Carl said, What are you going to do? Be quiet. Be quiet, Billy answered. Don't scare im. They walked carefully toward the steer making the same muffled cracking the steer had made. It stood staring at them between two saplings, low hanging fronds covered its body back of the head. When they had got very near to it, Billy put a hand on Carl's arm and they both stopped. Billy slowly shifted the flashlight to Carl who took it without a word, the beam still directed into the eyes of the young steer. Slowly and deliberately Billy raised his arm until the barrel of the .30-.30 was at the eye of the animal, and then he fired.

The shock seemed delayed. For a while it seemed that nothing whatever had happened. It was as if the smell of gunpowder, and the shaft of light, and the two columnar men and the mass of the animal floated together into one hanging moment, moving free from the earth. The report of the gun had removed all the tension of the presence they felt as they walked forward. The heavy mist fell. The wet hair of the animal slowly descended to earth, nestling itself upon the ever damp leaves. Oddly enough, Carl thought at that moment, there were no poisonous snakes west of the Cascades in Washington. There are no poisonous spiders either. There are mostly vegetative things this side of the mountains. No poisonous things . . . however the slugs are of great size, growing apparently on the vegetation to tremendous proportions, what *do* slugs live on, he asked himself. How do they grow to such fat dimensions. And then he saw the animal on the ground, thick blood was running out of its eye. Through the space of wet air one could feel the warm blood. The animal's hind legs were still scratching for the earth, they still sought their ground. The thin fallen branches trembled with the groping of the legs.

Billy split the skin around the hind quarters and with his foot placed squarely on the spine near the rear, broke it by a sudden snap, the two hooves in his hands. The front quarters were more difficult to get off because the head had to be removed. But in a surprisingly short time he had that part severed and they stood pointing the flashlight at what remained. Because Billy was the larger man he would attempt to carry the hind quarters. Carl asked Billy again in which direction he thought they should go. Billy studied for a moment. Then he pointed out the direction he thought they should take. By this time Carl had completely given up trying to figure it out on the basis of where he thought they had come from. He acquiesced completely.

They started out. Billy led with the crotch of the hind quarters around his neck, the hooves hanging down in front. He staggered under the load only when his footing was insufficient. Carl had a harder time. After a while, when crossing fallen logs that were large enough in circumference he tended to rest there, sitting under the weight, a comfortable, cold relief. At those times he asked Billy to wait. They went on and on. The two men got home by a route that would appear on paper as a long snaking curve, many switchbacks and some loops. But finally they drew near the pond of water. When they approached the marshes from a side Billy was unfamiliar with, he spoke hopefully that they were nearly there. They circled the small body of water and walked slowly into the second clearing. They set down their burdens and rested for the last time. They were wet through and through. Their necks were covered with thick blood that had grown cold. Blood ran down their backs. They were of course unaware of this. In the black night they had a rest, Carl smoked. Billy did not smoke. They talked of having a drink when they got back to the house. What did you think of that, Carl? he asked. I don't know, Carl answered, it seemed the thing to do. You know, Billy, how I have to explain these things to myself. I know that's absurd. We got the deer. What's the difference if it's a hereford. If you think that's my quarrel with life you're mistaken. The man who owns this animal, or what we have of it, is probably asleep in his bed right now, safe and sound, lying next to his wife. Or if not that, he's in a tavern somewhere with his hand on the ass of a bleary-eyed broad. It's not going to make any difference to him and he can be forgotten. And you can be forgiven,

Billy, for this small theft. I assure you it won't change the world. But there are better questions than that. Let's go.

The two men prepared to put their burdens on their shoulders and when they had struggled underneath them they started on. Shortly, around the last point of second growth, they saw the weak light from Billy's house.

THE END OF THE NIGHT

Billy put on a pot of coffee. Carl walked
ON INTO THE OTHER PART OF THE HOUSE. HE STOPPED
short, suddenly aware of people sleeping. The two
little boys were in their beds. Billy's wife was in the
double bed and she moved slightly, lifting her head,
but did not seem awake. Carl retreated to the kitchen.
Billy had built up the fire in the cookstove and put
some water on to heat. They would have to wash the
blood off themselves. The house was cold and damp.
They crept back into the main room and Billy put
some newspaper into the wood stove, and then some
fir scrap. The blaze started and then roared. Finally
it settled down to burning. There was a great deal of
smoke because the wood was wet, but it burned

• 183

brighter and he put more in. He stood back watching it, the crack in the lid on top let a shaft of flickering light onto his face. He was smiling slightly. He hooked his thumbs into his wide heavy belt and shifted his weight to one leg. They went back into the kitchen after the fire had got a good start. They washed themselves with warm water and soap. They finished off what was left of a pint of whiskey.

So, by the time I got to Valdez, Billy was saying, I didn't like Alaska. A very hard town, Valdez. I got passage from a guy in a small boat down to Sitka. I didn't like that either but I stayed there for a while. I always thought of Alaska I guess as a place where you hunted kodiak bears but I found out they were out in the Aleutians. I got a job delivering prescriptions for a druggist in Sitka. On my day off I walked out of town, usually, into the timber. It's on an island, Baranof . . . pretty big island . . . long . . . it's a long way around it. They stood warming their hands over the fire. That's a very rainy place. If you think it rains a lot here, you ought to go to southern Alaska. . . . it rains much more there. And the worst people in the world go there. Opportunists . . . they all think they'll get rich. They're all bitter . . . Oh, of course I don't know all of them, but the ones I knew. I thought Alaska was a new world, but it was just Wisconsin again. Colder in some places, wetter in others. I don't know what it was like when the Russians had it but when I got there it was the same old story. What did you expect? Carl asked absentmindedly, staring at the flickering cracks in the stove top.

Billy took a step back and looked up. I expected . . . what did I expect? I expected in the first place for there not to be many people. I expected to go to the interior, but I was told I couldn't possibly do that because I wasn't equipped. I don't know if that was true or not. But what the hell, you can't make your way around a place if you haven't got a way to do it. It's hard to get around in Alaska. It's closed off, it's a land of businessmen. Jesus, go to a store and they'd charge you twenty-five dollars for a cap. They'd laugh in your face if you didn't have the twenty-five. Everywhere I went I heard talk of how too many people who didn't have any money were coming to Alaska. They said, why are all you people coming up here, we haven't got anything for you. You think you can go to work making five hundred dollars a week. This was just after a bunch of men went up there to build government projects. But after all that work was over the men kept going up there thinking they would make a fortune. But the natives, shit, natives! They'd been there five years, they didn't like to see a bunch of people coming in with no money to buy anything.

I met a guy from Anacortes who got put off by a salmon boat at Sitka. I don't even think they were supposed to do that but the captain of the boat did it. He had been caught selling salmon, hell I don't even remember if it was salmon, it might have been sole or halibut, anyway it seems he was stationed at some kind of traps. Crabs? They're caught in traps. Ya. I think. Anyway, he sold some on the side. He said it was common practice, he just got caught. Anyway we started going around together. One day I was walking down on the dock and I heard these shots right next to me and he hollered to me to jump aboard this sailboat. He had the motor going and as we pulled away from the dock he kept shooting. I asked him what the hell was going on and he just said shut up! take 'er out, and he kept shooting. I saw a few guys standing on shore but they were just pointing. Well, anyway, the bastard had robbed the bank and stole a boat and all at once I was helping him. The thing I regretted most was I had a nice little girl in Sitka. It took the harbor patrol three days to catch us and by that time he had taken so many pot shots at them from behind trees and rocks it was hopeless for me. We sunk the boat the first day down the shore, the wind drove us on some rocks. I got two years for that and nobody would believe me. Two women said I wasn't at the bank with this guy. That's the only help I had. How do you like that!

Yes sir! The boyhood dream fulfilled. Come true! Absolutely teeroo! When they threw my ass in that prison, I'll tell you one thing, I cried. It took me many sad weeks to realize I had got to go to Alaska like I always wanted to and now I was walkin' in an exercise yard and a lot of mean lookin' cons were staring at me. An old man in there took me under his wing . . . he was very kind to me, I don't know what I'da done without him. He taught me to see that fate could have been a lot harder on me than she was. But I don't know. I don't know whether I can think like that either. It just might have been even too much for that judge to swallow after those two women said I wasn't with that guy. Yow, so he let me off easy. But that's why when I come on a nice fat little steer like tonight, I claim her. She's mine. I take her for another part of the wages somebody owes me, and I intend to go on collecting those wages the rest of my life. Whenever it's safe. Absolutely. And if I have to, when it's not safe. I'm just like those union officials—a petty thief. Last winter when we were hungry I walked into the supermarket and put a fifty pound bag of flour on my shoulder and walked right past the checker, I even smiled and said, Hello! He smiled back and asked me if I needed some help. I replied, no, I did not! As long as I can stand up I won't need any help. Of course if I couldn't stand up, that sonofabitch would be the last man on earth to ask if he could help!

The oldest boy staggered from his bed and went outside to the toilet. The two men stood with their backs to the stove. Billy's wife stirred under the covers, both men glanced in that direction.

Billy, what does it mean to you to live as you do here back in the woods, away from everything . . . well, I mean . . . I know that's important to you, for instance you were shocked I was working out of the employment agency, and we had a talk about that I remember. I know you have an integrity that McCarty hasn't, you'd never in the world work for Smith. But don't you think that a "steady job" in the long run would get your kids' teeth fixed, you worry a lot about that. So construction labor pays two ninety-five an hour. But you don't work that much more than I do and I work, it looks to me at least, I work say, three months out of the year. You probably work four or five. At the most. Now if it didn't bother you that your kids have bad teeth, if it didn't bother you, there wouldn't be anything to say about it I suppose. Billy was bending over the woodbox, he put a few pieces in the stove, carefully moving those that were embers and stacking the new ones in a criss-cross manner.

Ummmm. Where am I gonna get this steady job. I'm not saying I want a steady job because I think steady jobs are just another way of saying work more and get less and in the end you'll get a watch if you don't get fucked up. Look, I'm still young, I used to be a lot younger. Who wasn't? There was another thing I learned in that prison. When you get out, don't figure life like other people do. Who the hell could I convince I need a "steady job," who? And they're right, I am different. Whatever that means. And anyway, when you get out of prison you figure you're better than other people. Why not. I'm not talking about myself, I shouldn't have even been there, in every prison there are a lot of people who shouldn't be there, even by the standards of any pissyassed clothier downtown. I'm not talking about me. Oh christ no! Most of those men are there because they were *apprehended* for any everyday act. And those that are there for unusual crimes, like murder or something like that, they have more reason to be proud. Not of the crime, oh hell no, it's not any great thing to kill a man. But they've been sequestered, that's another word I learned. They're extraordinary, like Sir Isaac Shithead, the whole thing . . . the *night,* I bet you never saw the night from prison. Well, you don't know what it is. It isn't the same thing. When the sun comes up it comes up different in prison. The old man told me that too. He told me he'd been watching it for many years. It's closer in prison. When you're on the outside the sun is a long way off. There are many convicts in prisons all over this country that are awake right now. It's still dark but they're awake. A breeze when it comes up is something special if you're standin' by the window. It turns your head. Look, I went to prison, you went to college. It's the same difference. All that happened is that you got a little confused and I got cleared up. But we see the same things.

There was a silence, the sleeping people could be heard breathing. Billy poured the coffee from their cups back into the pot and set it on the stove.

It's a crummy school. Don't ever go there. I had only two years, of course five were hanging over my head. But I saw some of those guys, like the old man, lifers. You don't even know about that. You couldn't even talk to those men. And you're what's thought of as an intelligent man. You're not bad . . . you try to see the right side of things from the weak, helpless man's point of view. But you couldn't even get the old man to loosen up. He'd take you for some kind of untrustworthy nut. Billy looked over at the two children sleeping, and then stared at the flickering cracks in the stove top. But he wouldn't tell you nothing. He used to get into trouble because he sometimes got it into his head not to shave. It even seemed to bother the guards to slap him around. He spoke of his daughter very much. He'd left her in Washington and gone to Alaska. She must have been pretty little when he got sent up . . . he had a picture, oh I don't know, she looked six or seven. The minute he knew how long I was gonna be in, he started begging me to go see her when I got out. And I had two years at least. When you start asking someone two years ahead, and do it every day, you've got something on your mind. The patience! The hope! And the sight! I later asked other people there if he had asked them to see his daughter. There were very few. They were all long-termers. The wind started to come up. The house shook slightly. The wind could be heard in the old hemlock outside Billy's door.

Ya, in that territorial prison he watched for men he thought would go to see his daughter. She was six years old when he went in but he wasn't even sure about that. The sun gets to be very exact. It never fails, but all the other things. The moon inches up and down the bar all year long. He was a shrewd old man by that time, he went in late I think, but he made the change. The prison owed a lot to him. He met every new man with a good word, and continued to do so, unless they were too mean by the time they got there.

I mean, there's nothing you can say to a mean man. And all the time he thought his daughter was six years old. Well she wasn't. I guess I was the first one to do it. I looked her up. I got a boat and came on down. She was sixteen and had two kids. One an outright baby and the other was walking around starting to talk. The kids were by two different men. She had been staying with relatives for the past few years but when she had the first baby they kicked her out and she was on relief working for a farmer as a house girl. They had an arrangement. She didn't report that she was getting hers and the kids' meals for the work she did. The relatives didn't ever write the old man, thank god. She seemed a little bit off, like she had been in prison too. So I married her. Carl whistled low. Is that her? Yes, that's her, Billy said, and then he started to fix the fire again.

But did you love her? Carl said, and then answered before Billy could speak, No, of course. That wasn't the point.

So you know, it isn't a matter of how I feel about my kids' teeth. I mean I can't think like that any more. I know there's no responsibility I can live up to. I don't look right. My car looks stolen. My shoulder's fucked up. I fell out of a car when I was a kid. I slouch. I'm strong, but I look funny. I couldn't stick around on a steady job anyway. I was incarcerated.

That's what they call it. I don't mean to say I can explain everything by that. In the course of a life that's only an incident like any other thing. And if I wanted to apply myself I could live like anyone else. I wouldn't have to be married to a woman who is so dirty I feel funny inviting you here. I know she's got food all up and down the front of her dress. But she's good to the kids. She's not bitter. When the oldest kid starts to school you know what she wants, she wants the kid to have a dime a day to take to school so he won't be embarrassed. Jesus Christ! Hell no, I can't buy oranges! I stole the goddamn chainsaw, I cut wood to keep us warm. I stole the rifles! Hell, I bought the horse for the kids. I could have bought oranges. That's true, that's true. But I can't steal a horse—people are very touchy about that. So are kids. They want horses more than oranges. I mean their eyes light up when they go out to ride the horse but if it's just an orange, they just eat it; once when I bought a dozen oranges they threw some of them on the ground when they hadn't ate half of them. And I can't buy a dentist either! And I sure can't steal a dentist! I mean when those welfare workers told us we needed to see a dentist I wanted to choke their fat throats! I really did want to kill them. I wanted to tear their asses off! Because you know what they told my wife? They told her that since I make two ninety-five an hour they couldn't help the kids. And when my wife said to them but he's always out of work, they just stared at her and said I needed to work more. Ha! ha! Citizens, lend me your ears. I can't even live with myself since I didn't shoot em down like dogs, in the back, as they went to get in their state car.

The cold light of early spring came up over the forest outside the house. The two men talked on, earnestly sometimes, now and then laughing. Oh to hell with it, Carl said. He got up and put on his coat. But you remember Carl, you be there next Monday morning. We'll get on that job together. When I talked to the dispatcher he thought they'd be calling up a lot of men. If it comes through it ought to pay a lot of money. Tunnel work's a higher rate. O.K., I'll be there, Carl said, as they were at the door. He walked down the steps and then went toward the car. There was a grey light everywhere now, the barn could be seen in dull outline. The forest stood quietly dark, the tops of the trees bending in the misty breeze.

Prologue to the Tunnel

Late winter is the season of hard luck. In
THAT SEASON, IN THE NORTH, THE STRANGE PEOPLE
show themselves. Poor workers come into a tavern with
the black of coal soot on their faces. There may be one
with the black of nightfighting under his eyes, and he
may have on a hat of civil war. He may be followed
by an older man with a rough cap, wearing dark
glasses. Their faces will be dark with the dirt of that
underground thing. But they will be the deliverers, not
the diggers. Not the real thing. Never the real thing.
Any necessity in our day seems contrived. Phoenix may
complain in the winter because so many of the
irresponsible seek her. But they are a different breed.
Those who stay north of the clemency are truly men

who live in the sense of the everyday. One day true, is like another, but they have an attachment, if you take it that way. They cannot be gone, from one season to another. They stay, and the birds come and go. It never matters. If you take it from the dull, cold, grey corners of the streets of Duluth where the blue lake appears down every upgoing street, the long slim ore boats come from the east in the spring to rest there. An arrival. You go to Bismarck. Farm machinery suddenly, long rows of streets with metal combines standing in cold yards. Waiting on summer, to be sold. And then on across the plains of the anaconda, that long, vicious snake which crushes the life out of its victims. Down in the mines of Butte men laugh and weep in their own endless winter. And so to Washington. The old crippled Wobbly walks down the street, his head against the rainy wind, his cork boots worn to nothing. He wears a stiff canvas jacket with a double back. Frayed into strings at the cuff. A white beard. A brown cigarette. Turning a corner his eyes rush open in the new wind off the islands in the Sound. Men who are outside must have that interest. There must be a question they ask. Whether they do or not is of no importance. Their presence, if they are not established, asks it. In the north there is only one thing. The Spring. Anyone who denies this has taken up other securities.

In the early spring, in western Washington, on the corner of a small town at the mouth of a river on the Sound, two men met. They greeted each other and stood for a while. One was smoking a cigarette. He was dressed in a large long wool coat from a second-hand store, on his feet he wore uninsulated rubber boots, their tiestrings hanging loose down across the uppers. He waved the cigarette in the air and laughed. The air was filled with moisture and the two men huddled in their coats as if they needed them. Both men wore headgear. The man who was smoking wore a cloth cap with the ear flaps hanging down, and when he turned his head the flaps blew in the wind, their strings standing far out. The other man wore a tin hat. He was not quite so tall as the man who was smoking. Heavier. He looked like a strong man, but he had a lopsidedness to his carriage. There was something wrong with his shoulder. He had on boots. They looked like army boots, a leather tab around the laces at the top. Otherwise he had on that rain gear workers wear in the northwest, a short rubber coat, and rubber pants which, up under the coat, were a bib affair, like a farmer's overalls.

They started walking down the street. When they got to the union hall they went in through the narrow door. There were many men inside the hiring hall. They had gone through a passageway with a window in it, and had sat down in the seats. Billy went to the window and talked to the man. He returned and sat down next to Carl. He said we should stick around a while, he's making out the slips, but we're on our way.

THE TUNNEL

It would be a while before the work in
THE TUNNEL STARTED. IN THE MEANTIME THEY RAN
carriages far across a system of wooden ramps to a wall
that was being built against the swift river, dumping
cement into the forms. The route lay over the churn-
ing tailwater which roared out of a wide gallery at the
bottom of the powerhouse. They did this carting for
a week or so then Billy was moved to the day shift.
Carl continued to work the second shift, beginning at
four o'clock in the afternoon. Again, this was a short-
lived arrangement. When the main tunnel from the
dam to the powerhouse was drained, a new concrete
apron for the tailwater was laid out to the wall and
the river. Carl's work consisted mostly of tending

a huge pump the crane had let down into the hole. There was much water from the diverted river coming in there. So another week went by. Carl and Billy talked every day. There was a little lapover of their shifts. Sometimes they exchanged gossip about the other workers they had met on the job. There was always the speculation as to when they would start working in the tunnel. They looked forward to it with an apprehensive excitement. The hours would be shorter. A six hour day. And a higher rate of pay. The grouting foreman and the engineers and officials were making trips back to the main tunnel head to check the damage and inspect the work. It was said that this was the first time the main tunnel and penstocks had been shut down since 1938.

Men in the lowest position are usually uninformed as to the nature of the work they do, especially in construction. They had been able to learn very little of what they would be doing. Some information filtered down through the hierarchy of officials and engineers and surveyors through the carpenters and machine operators. True, laborers are generally less capable men when it comes to that sort of comprehension. From force of habit they have learned that they will be told at the last moment when to go to work, and at the last moment when they are no longer needed, in other words, you need not return tomorrow. Or on Monday, the usual case. It is also true they are kept standing about a great deal of the time. This requirement is the most difficult of all the situations a laborer has to put up with. On a highly mechanized project the carpenter is the only man who has a great deal of real, manual work. The laborer on the other hand is traditionally expected to look as though he is indeed working and when a foreman comes around he tries to look busy. If he is so brazen as to fly in the face of this rule, he is either asking to be fired, or he is in a good position with the powers that be. Usually this situation is no one's fault. There are times the company needs many men to do strictly non-skilled, physical work. When there is nothing at all to do the man is expected to develop that skill which shows a busyness when no actual work is being done. Men who run machines do not have this problem. They are an extension of the machine, and when the machine is idle, the man who runs it is expected to be idle too.

Where are the engineers? The experts in khaki pants, these days of labor? Are they in their little plywood shacks at their drawing boards? How cowardly! Why don't they take a walk down to the site and instruct the people who would all have their caps off with attention. One speaks of "education" for adults and children. Instead of endlessly disposing of people as materials, it might do well to show them, for instance, the workings of a hydroelectric power system. This would not be too difficult since the system is near at hand and the largest class of ignorant workers have time to waste. Obviously, apart from the very interesting business of how water produces power, it would relieve those workers of the necessity to perform the rite of acknowledged cheating, for which they are in every respect expected to hold the bag. It would relieve the pressure, relieve and correct their sense of false presence, which relief is needed, false presence being one of the most prevalent of modern diseases. In effect, this planned policy to sequester men from work they are on the other hand forced to do, is one of the primary aims of the modern state: it is a planned murder beside which war is of little consequence. But in a world in which populations grow much faster than real work, such disclosures become pointless. As the world's cognizance, both technological and human, becomes greater, it ought to be able also to pause, and give that instruction which makes men feel less isolated from their surroundings. A state with a heart, if such a proposition seems reasonable, would naturally be concerned with those men who are least able to understand anything. The rarefied hauteur of the informed is a condition that has proven more dangerous than valuable. Universities in this respect are wholly caged by the state. Their artificiality comes not from the nature of what they try to show, but from their partiality. A human ailment. The state has no excuses.

In the powerhouse there were four bays and four generators. Generators can be separated into two common types. Those with their shafts horizontal. Those with their shafts vertical. The generators in this particular powerhouse were of the first kind. Generally, now, unless some special problem presents itself, or unless the height of the dam merits it, horizontal shafts are not installed. The power connection with the horizontally oriented generator is made from the lake through a main tunnel and penstocks which lead off of that. Each steel enclosed wheel at the end of the horizontal shaft has its heavy lugs engaged by the tremendous pressure of a penstock. Into this powerhouse, with its four generators, ran eight penstocks.

All the penstocks had been drained along with the main tunnel. The generators were not to be overhauled, but they were shut down because with the draining of the tubes there was now no pressure whatsoever. The thing to be fixed lay at the very head of the main tunnel, up under the headgate. The distance was very hard to calculate. The plans gave exactly seven hundred and eighty-three feet from generator to main tunnel head. The first trip Billy and Carl made back to the work area seemed approximately a half a mile. They entered the first small tunnel, the penstock, through a hole halfway up the wheel casing. A heavy, bolted plate had been removed. They climbed up a stepladder and went through feet first onto a stepladder on the inside. Immediately inside the casing hung a weak raw light bulb. They had flashlights. Billy had trouble getting in the hole. His large belly would just barely squeeze through. Jesus Christ! I hope I can get back outa here, he said looking at Carl, his face flushed. He laughed. Carl climbed up and got into the hole and went down the ladder. All the men wore rubber boots.

The tunnel led endlessly into a receding dark hole. There were six men, including the grouting foreman, for that shift. There was about ten inches of running water in the bottom of the penstock. The penstock was seven foot in diameter, Carl judged from his own height—the ceiling was about a foot above his head. Whew! Billy said. Goddamn it's dark in here even with the flashlights. You could smile your ass off and nobody'd know it! The men waded through the water. The yellow light back at the generator got very pale. Finally it was nearly impossible to see it. There was a turning in the penstock and shortly after that they entered a larger tunnel.

The diameter increased to about twelve feet. They passed the mat, dark, bent ellipticals of other penstock entrances. And then this tunnel came to an end. With an oblique turn they entered the main tunnel and total blackness. Sharp reverberating noises came from the lower end. They turned their backs on the noise and started for the tunnel head. In their relayed conversation as they walked in single file very close to each other, it was learned that the work at the other end was a vertical shaft being tunneled to the surface. No one seemed to be able to explain its purpose. One of the men had seen the staging, built higher and higher as the men worked up, and he thought that the terrific noise came from the men dropping things. It was an anxious question because it had scared all of them except the foreman. The depth of water increased to a little over a foot in the main tunnel. And now they must be coming to a slight turn because there was a greater flow of reverberant noise, and they could begin to see a light.

When at last they arrived at the tunnel head, Billy shouted into Carl's ear. There was difficulty hearing because at the tunnel head, which joined the vertical access tunnel to the lake, the leakage from the shutoff descended with the force and roar of a gale coming straight down. Hell, *that's* why there's so much water running through there! Billy shouted. Ya, are you cold? Cold as hell, Billy answered. Their black wool underwear could not keep back the chill. The temperature in the tunnel was above freezing. But it was in the middle thirties, and given the saturation of the air, they shivered in jerks and began to look around for something to do to keep warm. There was nothing. The grouting foreman was having trouble with the pressure hoses. Grout is a thin, gruel-like cement which can be pumped through hoses or dry packed. It sets extremely hard and fast. It will set in water.

They were again standing around with nothing to do. Occasionally they were required to move or adjust some shoring. But that was all, the rest of the time that first night they just stood around shivering. The grouting foreman was very busy, but really he was doing little except to run around looking at the gauges or putting his gloved hand on the prop that held the mouth of the hose against the tunnel wall. On the ceiling of the tunnel for a space of twenty or thirty feet there were holes about three inches across. From these holes sprung streams of great force. It would not do to get in front of one. This was the trouble. The tunnel was old and had developed leaks through its metal lined concrete shell. The job was to run grout into these holes until the cavity in the earth outside the tunnel was filled. This might take weeks. It was predicted by the engineers on the basis of the force and quantity of the water that some of the cavities might be as large as a medium-sized house. The pressure from the entering water was ninety pounds to the square inch. Grout was being pumped at one hundred and five pounds. This was a slow exchange. And sometimes the pressure on both sides varied. Headway was lost. The grout was being mixed and forced from the outside. Far outside the tunnel, straight through under the vertical shaft being raised, the men and pumps worked.

After they received their first check, they were not so anxious to go to work each day. There grew up a feeling that the work was not too highly paid at all. For all the men, except the foreman, who was a veteran, the walk back to the tunnel head was more difficult each day. The foreman was slightly rummy they thought. Their nerves could never get used to the sharp, endlessly ricocheting sounds that traveled through the tunnels. A sound might have an innocent origin, an instrument so small as a hammer, dropped on the staging, would haunt the shafts for a full minute. The original blow repeated itself again and again. A crowbar was matter for terror. If he drops that fucking crowbar I'll killim! Billy would shout, if

he saw the foreman using the crowbar. The sound
was so compressing and exhausting, with the end of
the shift the men would struggle down the current of
the main tunnel in and out of zones of full sound and
at last crawl up out of the penstock through the hole
in the wheel casing to stand on the immaculate floor
of the powerhouse staring at each other like
shipwrecks washed at last upon an island. They
milled, dripping wet, dazed, as if they had no bearing.
Out into the cold black they would walk across the
gravel fill outside.

Sometimes now, Billy stopped at Carl's house
before going home. Sometimes they would stop by for
Mary and take her to the WhileAway for a few beers.
From this workless work they were exhausted. They
would for the most part sit limp in the booths and
listen to the questions Mary put about the work or the
reports of her day at home. Hey, Billy said, you
know that thing they call cla-cla-claustrophobia? I
think I got it! Maybe I've always had it. I never been
in a place like that since I was born. Carl said it might
be true, but if he really had it, he probably wouldn't
even be able to go down there every day. Perhaps one
could have a touch of it. Carl thought that because he
could go into the tunnel but it made him very
nervous. And he thought he was seeing things a lot of
the time. The vibrations terrified him so much he had

208 •

several times involuntarily started to run for the generator. But he said that each time this happened he laughed at himself because there was no possible chance a man could make it from the tunnel head if the water started to break away at the gates above. He told them that with each step toward the generator, and with each sound, with each seeming new rush of water, he kept asking himself if he could make it from that point. Ya, and you know what that foreman said the other day, Billy said. Those gates at the top are old and rotten. I asked him if he thought they'd break. He said naw! gates older than that hold, and then he went into all the old gates he'd worked underneath. He did admit there was a grouting crew that got sort of suffocated in a tunnel he worked on in Oregon. But he said that wasn't on his shift. I suppose we're supposed to take that as a good omen! We're supposed to think his ass's charmed!

But in spite of the uneasiness, they went through the hole day after day. Billy had a habit of looking around the powerhouse and then out through its towering roman arched windows to the bank of dark firs across the river. It happened that as they were quitting one night a particularly rolling and unexpected sounding shouldered its way up and down the main tunnel. The shocks were so pressing and sharp on the nervous system Carl had several times jerked forward on the brink of a full run. He felt like a fool and looked around with a short laugh. The little group of men sloshed on through the water toward their penstock. They entered the feeder tunnel and their lights probed the walls for the second penstock. It would be a time-consuming mistake to enter the wrong one. They had told themselves that the walk in and out would be a waste of time, but they were as a matter of fact, deeply afraid of coming up against a closed generator. Stopped at an end with no exit. But of course, all that was foolish. The foreman trusted it. After all he was an experienced man, he had worked in many tunnels. And the officials had been in there. They were very careful men. They had spent two hours one afternoon, casually looking it over. But if the thing happened it could happen one time as well as another.

Spring wore on. In the mountains, there was no more wet snow on the boughs of the trees. A new green. They made the trip up the river passing the small grubby little "ranches" with their pastures full of high cedar and hemlock stumps. The job was lasting longer than they had expected. The men were growing used to the noises. They were not so disturbed by the long walk in to the work and they told themselves they did not get quite so cold anymore. They wore more than one suit of wool underwear. This special clothing made them more awkward than ever walking up the gentle elevation to the tunnel head. After one especially cold Friday night, they had stayed two hours overtime because the last shift would not be coming on. Their nerves were a little rawer than usual and a great crash came suddenly on the little group making its way at last into the joint of the penstock and as a group they shot forward. All of them stumbling at once, the forward members fell down in the rush. They got up and ran, the noise was still coming. The walls of the tunnel seemed on the verge of collapse with the recurring sound. In the minds of the men there was a wall of water, the first great dark wave from the lake, coming after them, somewhere back of them. It was rushing forward and they conceived that they would rise on it, and the second wave which would come shortly after, would crush their heads against the overhead steel of the penstock suffocating them with one blow. It was a lack of air and breath that they most feared. When they got to the ladder and the weak bulb they knew it had not happened and they laughed at themselves nervously, goosing each other up the ladder to the light of the powerhouse. They all left together and on the way home stopped in a very bright

• 211

fluorescent lit restaurant, before starting the long trip down the valley.

It was a Tuesday, fifteen minutes before they went into the tunnel the crew stood around the immaculate generator. Billy Hendersson was standing with his thumbs in his belt, chewing on a toothpick. He even wore his hard hat into the tunnel. It always clanged against the side of the steel opening as he backed down the inside ladder. The other four men on the crew were older than Billy and Carl. They had grey stubble beards. About five minutes before the time to start they grew restless and started saying the usual things—well, I guess we have to get our asses in there, if we get all the way in, do you think we'll get all the way out?

They entered the penstock and proceeded up to the feeder tunnel. Billy and Carl were talking about a carpenter they had just talked to outside. They were laughing. The carpenter was a character. He always said, if you asked him for a cigarette, or a ride, or any other small favor, Be my guest! He wore eggshell white bib overalls and an old style sheepskin-lined aviator's cap.

It was an especially dull night. They had become so used to the sounds they were bothered by them again. Billy by this time was threatening the grouting foreman outright, to his face, and before he had even picked up a heavy tool. There were very few spouting holes left. All of the leaks were not independent. As some of the cavities were filled with grout, unions were formed and several holes would be plugged with one injection.

The shift ended. They collected all the tools for the last shift and climbed down from the staging to the tunnel floor. They were in the rushing water coming down from the leaking gates. They started walking, the floodlights at the staging receded behind them, growing dimmer as they walked into the hollow circular darkness of the tunnel ahead. They were cold. Billy turned and said to Carl who was behind him, You know that shaft they're driving down at the end of this tunnel, well, you know a kid was killed on that the other day. He fell right down through it. I don't know if it was all the way but they said he was pretty fucked up.

All of the men were thinking of the moment they would stick their heads through the hole into the powerhouse. There was an anxiety to be out of it once the trip was begun. Standing around the head Carl had devised a solitude, a faith that the gates above would hold and that the torrent of rain through the fittings was natural. He had rationalized that this was the maximum shut off and it was probably true of all such hydroelectric dams. He had come to know that all "conditions" for that kind of work were deceiving.

Just then an overhead section of the vertical shaft, weighing about a ton, let loose and traveled down through the successive platforms of the staging like a shell. The shocks began in rings of force up the circular tunnel walls, and very quickly they were there and back. The men stopped, fixed like a bronze group. They turned backward and then forward as one thing. The sound had returned and gone again several times in that space. Men's reflexes are very slow. The tunnel waxed full with shattering sound, and then in an instant the men started forward like a caterpillar moving its joints across a length of broken ground. They stumbled and some ran over the ones in front. The line was dissolved. They were a shifting ground, running onward to what they thought was their penstock, in a foot of water heavy around their feet. The gates had broken. The men were caught midwaist by the first wave, and there were groans and a quickening of their throats. But no screams. Their arms splashed in the rising water. They were swept as it happened down to the last penstock and those ahead saw the weak light by the ladder. Now they all splashed like rats and tried to find any hold on the ground they could. One of the group, a large man, who had been leading the way with a flashlight, was far ahead. Another wave caught them raising them higher in the tunnel so they had to duck their heads to keep from banging on the ceiling. Carl thought he heard Billy's cap strike the steel top of the tunnel. They were shouting now. That gate broke! We're goners. Hurry up! the man in the lead shouted.

Carl had passed Billy in the tunnel, he never knew how. Whether he had run around or over him he never knew. But by the time he got to the ladder he had swallowed a lot of water, and could hardly make his muscles move. Every time he reached for the ladder he was drawn by a backwash away. The first man was out and had his face sticking back through the hole shouting, You better get the fuck outa there! He was screaming. Carl waited. He had got his hand on the ladder. Another man came up. He climbed up the ladder. Where was Billy. Where were the two old men. He felt a hand on his leg and then a smiling red face shot up above the water. Whew! Let's get outa here, Billy said. Carl went up the ladder. He stood on the floor and saw Billy's head appear through the hole. Billy was trying to squeeze out. A wave of full pressure then came down the fully choked barrel of the penstock and there was a subtle and terrible vibration of strength the men had never heard or felt before and it held the grip on the powerhouse like a hand holds the lever of a powerful machine. As Billy Hendersson was trying to get out the hole it caught him like the wadding in a gun. He was shot up into the air and out through the many panes of the vaulted window, on a sudden column of water.

FALL

Carl stood by the fence watching a group
OF KILLDEER IN THE FIELD. JAMES WAS IN A TREE NEARBY
throwing apples into a sheet on the ground. The
children ran around the house. The McCartys were
going to move soon. Back to the camp. James was
going to work for Smith. The income tax refund they
had counted on so much never came. Carl read in the
paper that a ring of thieves were operating in the
neighborhood, taking refund checks out of rural
mailboxes. The McCartys decided that was what
happened to their check. And then one evening during
the summer the McCartys, accompanied by The Old
Man, staggered out of The Savoy into their car. Going
out along the highway James drove exceptionally slow.

A highway patrolman noticed them and pulled them over. They were all so drunk they were nearly asleep. James was taken to the county jail. There was a fine of one hundred and fifty dollars or ninety days in jail. The Wymans at that time did not have the money to give them. Carl was out of work again. The only recourse was for James to bind himself over to Smith. Smith came, wrote a check, and the next day James reported for work with his carpenter's apron on, his hat straight on his head. His normally ready smile was not hesitant.

The two men carried in the apples to spread them on the floor of the upstairs room. All around the walls were James' ancient typewriters, small armatures, radios that did not work, his infinite gear. There was the mingled smell of old machines and stored apples. They spread the apples out and then went down to join the women sitting around the stove. It was a chilly day. They were all a little sad. Carl had already offered to haul some things in his old pickup. He did not use it for anything much now. James said that Smith would let him use one of his trucks. Carl encouraged him to make the move without Smith's help if possible, pointing out that it would do James no good at all to become any more beholden to Smith than he already was.

Ramona sat hunched over, smoking a cigarette

she had just rolled. She was perhaps the saddest of anyone about going back to the camp. It was a matter of shame to her. She was pregnant. The baby was due to arrive very soon, possibly within the next two weeks. Still, she smiled and laughed often, for she was amused often. She found very many things funny. She said with a slight smile to Mary, I guess I'm going to work in the field for that asshole Smith. Oh, you aren't either! Mary said. Yes I am. I've got to. It will take James forever to work off that hundred and fifty. But Ramona, you might have the baby in the field. You mean you're going to do the cutting back? Yes. That's what they're doing now. The children passed by smiling, eating apples. They skipped on out the door.

Ramona talked on aimlessly. She mentioned that she wanted to go to Seattle. A short argument followed between her and James. She wanted to try to get the children again. James had thought that a good idea when they first moved into the house, but didn't see the sense in it now they were going back to the pea-shack.

Ramona insisted. She said quietly, It will be all right. Carl mentioned that they were thinking of leaving that part of the country as soon as they could see their way. They did not know when, perhaps in a month or two, but certainly by the first of the year.

The McCartys were surprised, and disappointed, but had to agree that if they could they would leave too. James talked of going to California sometime. But the possibility of leaving that winter, for the McCartys, was gone now.

They moved back to the pea-shack. The Wymans did not see them for a while after that. A strangeness had grown up between the two families. When Ramona's baby came, Mary wanted very much to take some clothes she had made for it out to the camp. But she had the definite feeling Ramona would prefer she did not. That shame Ramona spoke of so often had grown overpowering. One night sometime after Ramona had taken the baby home from the hospital, she was in town with The Old Man. When they had spent all their money at The Savoy, they took a cab to the Wymans. Carl paid the driver and Ramona stumbled blindly into the house. The Old Man walked steadily but not always in the right direction. Carl helped him up the steps.

It happened that the Wymans had a visitor, a poet who had come up from Seattle to see Carl. He had a beard and spoke in a loud, arrogant voice. The poet found many things wrong with the world. And he expressed himself freely, as though his experience and learning could carry him even into areas that were foreign to him. They all sat at the round table in the Wymans' kitchen. The Old Man dropped into the rocking chair by the fire and went to sleep. The cat jumped into his lap and curled up. Pierce, the poet, was talking about Paris to Carl. Ramona and Mary were talking between themselves. Ramona was telling Mary that she had gone down to Seattle that morning to try to get the kids and that there seemed no hope at all now, the welfare people said the children were happy in their homes, attachments had been formed and that the families had adopted them. Ramona's consent was not needed because she was considered derelict. Pierce overheard the last of this and broke in, What do you mean? They can't do that! Ramona turned a bleary gaze on him as if she had just discovered him. She stared at him for some time. He asked, in a lower voice now, How old are they? POOP! she said in a low steady voice. Poop on you! Poop to you, you poop. Pierce withstood this barrage like a man. He settled back into this chair and looked from Ramona to Carl and from Carl to Ramona. I'm sorry, he said, very deferentially. Sure, you're a poop! The animation of this conversation, though not loud, had awakened The Old Man, and he sat forward with a vacant smile on his face and said, Hello, this is a mighty nice ice cream parlor you have here! and then went back to sleep. The cat stood up, arched its back and recurled itself on his lap.

• 221

Since the Wymans' truck had to be cranked, Pierce offered to take Ramona and The Old Man out to the camp when they were ready to go. Not long afterward, he took them home and then drove back to Seattle.

Winter came and then it was nearly Christmas. James stopped by the Wymans one afternoon on his way home. Mary had made some ginger cookies and he ate a few, talking rapidly about the days when his family drove the Auburn up to Vancouver Island from Hollywood, in the summertime. The next day would be Christmas Eve. The Wymans told him they planned to make the trip out to the pea-shack with some things for the children, and James said they would be home. They drove out into the brush to see Billy Hendersson first. It was a dark rainy night. Billy had been out of the hospital for some time. Carl wanted to tell him that he was leaving the pickup truck for him when they left, and that he should make arrangements to have someone get it at the railroad station in Cedar Mills. The Wymans would have to drive it to the train. Billy spent most of his time in bed these days. Under the covers, trying to keep warm. A wet chill went all through the house. All their wood was wet. Carl carried some more in from the shed and stacked it as near the stove as he thought safe. One of Billy's legs had been crushed and was put back together with pins and wires. His face had changed a great deal. His nose, which had been round and up-turned, was now straighter and thinner. He did not look the same, and Carl always had a strange feeling hearing the voice of the man he knew, come out of a different face. They made some coffee. It was instant coffee. There were several large jars left. The last time the two men were together Carl had to stop at the frozen food locker and as they came out through the passageway at the side of the store, Billy picked up a case of instant coffee and limped out with it under his arm. There was no expression on his face as Carl held the door for him.

The cold rain crept into the house. The Henderssons had no Christmas tree so it was a particular pleasure to the Wymans that they had brought one. On the tree they had hung pieces of candy and some cookies. They had a few presents for the children. The two men talked quietly, going over the last few things they had to say to each other. The children played and talked on the army cots. Finally the Wymans took their leave.

And they did not stay long at the McCartys. The rain had settled down to that steady descent. The fine rain. There was no wind, even in the tops of the tall evergreens. From the lights of the truck the road, the roadsigns, the telephone wires, shone. All glistening wet, and cold. The Wymans arrived home and put the children to bed. All three families settled down within the cold heart of that raining country. Out in the Sound the ferry boats drove through the rain. The constant passengers from the islands sat aboard. The old woman's rooster crowed, even in the middle of the night.

One morning, when the rain had turned to snow, five people stood on the platform with their baggage. Some of it had been checked, but they carried most of their possessions. The three children were all laden with bags, and boxes held by the strings. The man carried three suitcases, one under his arm, two in his hands. The children leaned out over the track looking to see if the train was coming. The mother pulled them back. Carl wondered if the two men would be in the house and worried about their dividing the blankets properly. He spoke of it to Mary. She had a faraway look in her eye and said she didn't know. The children saw the train coming down the track and then slow to a stop. Then they all got on and the train pulled out.

Printed July 1991 in Santa Barbara & Ann
Arbor for the Black Sparrow Press by Graham
Mackintosh & Edwards Brothers Inc. Text set in
Sabon by Words Worth. Design by Barbara Martin.
This edition is published in paper wrappers;
there are 300 hardcover trade copies;
150 hardcover copies have been numbered & signed
by the author; & 26 copies handbound in boards
by Earle Gray are lettered & signed by the author.

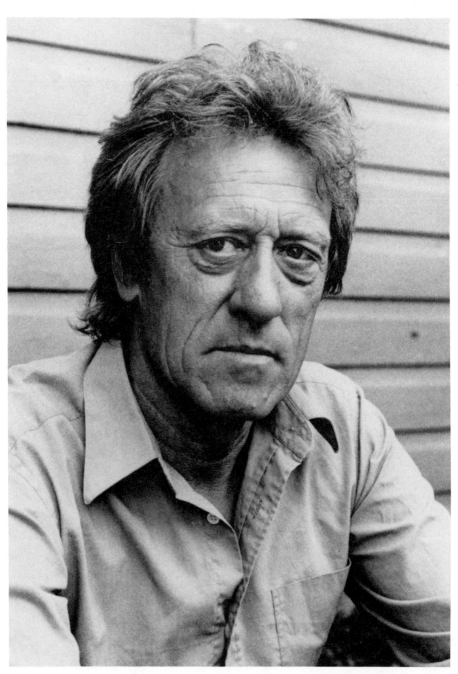

Photo: Chris Felver

EDWARD DORN was born in 1929 and grew up in Eastern Illinois, on the banks of the river Embarrass (a tributary of the Wabash). He never knew his father. His mother was of French ancestry, his grandfather a railroad man. He attended a one room school, while in high school played billiards with the local undertaker for a dime a point, and after two years at the U. of Illinois and two stops at Black Mountain College, traveled through the trans-mountain West following the winds of writing and employment. From 1965 to 1970 he lived in England, where he lectured at the U. of Essex. He has since lived and taught in Kansas, Chicago and San Francisco; throughout the 1980s he has taught in the Creative Writing Program of the U. of Colorado, Boulder, and, with his wife Jennifer Dunbar Dorn, edited the newspaper *Rolling Stock*. His major works include *The Newly Fallen, Hands Up!, Geography, Recollections of Gran Apacheria, Gunslinger, Hello La Jolla, Yellow Lola* and *Abhorrences* (poetry), and *By the Sound, Some Business Recently Transacted in the White World* and *The Shoshoneans* (prose).